"When God says no, he is extending an invitation to deeper intimacy, as Blake Long takes us in his new book, *Taking No for an Answer*. With careful and biblical insight, and with meaningful personal stories, Blake helps us see the deepest prayer life is not about using God, but about knowing him."

Jared C. Wilson, Assistant Prof. and Author in Residence at Midwestern Baptist Theological Seminary, author of *Love Me Anyway*

"I have always hated it when God tells me no, through a slammed door, a rejection letter, or a pink slip and I'm not sure anyone does. How do we respond when our lives take turns we didn't anticipate? How do we react when our dreams are crushed? When we suffer loss? Blake Long walks us through the pages of Scripture and helps us to see that God's 'no' is often a 'yes' to something better. If you are having a hard time trusting God in the dark, if you are confused and afraid by what you are seeing around you, this book helps you find your way back to faith again."

Daniel Darling, Director of the Land Center for Cultural Engagement and bestselling author of several books, including, *The Dignity Revolution*, *A Way With Words*, and *The Characters of Christmas*

"With wisdom and compassion, Blake Long helps us see the goodness of God's "no" as he equips readers to discern when to persevere in prayer and when he might be redirecting us. This is a message I wish I had heard as a new believer. It's one I still need to remember today. And it's one I'm sure will bless you in the days after you read this book."

Aaron Armstrong, author of *I'm a Christian—Now What?: A Guide to Your New Life with Christ*

"Prayer is hard, especially when our prayers seem to go unanswered. In *Taking No for An Answer*, Blake Long shares from his own experience, and points us to God's goodness and grace even when He says no. Biblical, practical, and hopeful, this book will help you grow in prayer."

Darryl Dash
Pastor, Liberty Grace Church; author of *8 Habits for Growth*

"Unanswered prayer can make or break our faith. Blake Long has put together a fantastic guide to build our faith when God doesn't answer us in the way we want. It's personal, practical, and deeply encouraging. Every Christian would benefit from reading this book and taking its message to heart."

Kevin P. Halloran, Project Manager at Open the Bible, author, *When Prayer Is a Struggle*

"Every Christian has struggled with seemingly unanswered prayer. In his new book *Taking No for An Answer: How to Respond When God Says No to Our Prayers*, Blake Long encourages us in our prayer lives when we don't get the answers from God that we think we want/need. Filled with theology and worship, Long's concise book will aid you in trusting God in all his sovereign answers to your prayers. Buy this book, and worship your God!"

Dr. Ed Romine, Pastor of Education and Evangelism, at First Baptist Church of Provo, Utah; itinerant preacher, evangelist.

TAKING NO
FOR AN ANSWER

*How to Respond When God
Say No to Our Prayers*

BLAKE LONG

THEOLOGY & LIFE
Applying theology to life

Copyright © 2022 Blake Long

All rights reserved. No part of this book may be reproduced in any form without permission from the author.

ISBN: 979-8-218-09181-1

First Edition

Scripture quotations are from The Holy Bible, English Standard Version® (ESV®), Copyright © 2001 by Crossway, a publishing ministry of Good News Publishers. All rights reserved.

Scripture quotations marked (NIV) are taken from the Holy Bible, New International Version®, NIV®. Copyright © 1973, 1978, 1984, 2011 by Biblica, Inc.™ Used by permission of Zondervan. All rights reserved worldwide. www.zondervan.com. The "NIV" and "New International Version" are trademarks registered in the United States Patent and Trademark Office by Biblica, Inc.™

Scripture quotations marked (NLT) are taken from the Holy Bible, New Living Translation, copyright ©1996, 2004, 2015 by Tyndale House Foundation. Used by permission of Tyndale House Publishers, Carol Stream, Illinois 60188. All rights reserved.

Cover and interior design: John Manning

Editor: Alex Duke

Contents

Foreword | Tim Challies	9
Introduction	11
1. The God Who is Attentive	
He Hears, Listens, & Inclines	23
2. Unanswered Prayer in the Bible	
God Said No to David, Paul, & Jesus	33
3. Lord, I Trust You	
Responding with Trust	47
4. Lord, All I Need is You	
Responding with Contentment	55
5. Lord, Forgive Me	
Responding with Repentance	67
6. Lord, I Won't Stop Praying	
Responding with Persistence	77
7. Lord, I Will Draw Near	
Responding with Coming Closer to God	87
8. Lord, Thank You	
Responding with Thankfulness	95
9. Lord, I Will Wait for You	
Responding with Patience	105
10. Lord, Sanctify Me	
The Prayer God Always Answers	119
Conclusion | Our Good, His Glory	127
Acknowledgements	131
Bibliography	133

To Jovi and Piper...
You two make life so fun
I pray you both come to know Jesus and find
ultimate satisfaction in Him

Foreword

THERE ARE TIMES when it seems like God does not hear us. There are times when it seems like God has become deaf to our prayers and unresponsive to our cries. There are times when we seek but do not find, knock but do not find the door opened. Why is it that God sometimes does not answer our prayers? And how should we respond when all we perceive is silence?

These are questions every Christian finds himself asking at one time or another—questions many wrestle with in times of great uncertainty or times of severe pain. Thankfully, these are questions we can take before the Lord and questions he is faithful to address in his Word.

You may find answers to some of your questions in the pages of Taking No for an Answer. Blake Long cannot tell you why God is silent in the particular circumstance that is grieving you right now, but he can tell you why God sometimes chooses not to answer our prayers (or at least not to make those answers immediately apparent) and he can reassure you that it is often far better this way.

Best of all, he can point you to the character of the God who loves you, who has saved you by his grace, and whose heart is always tenderly inclined toward you. He can point you to the Father who loves you as a precious child and who is every bit as compassionate in his "no" as in his "yes."

Tim Challies
Author of *Seasons of Sorrow* and
Blogger at challies.com

Introduction

Two Stories of Unanswered Prayer

I KNOW THE PAINS of unanswered prayer. All Christians do. When God throws a wrench in our timing or brings affliction to our lives, the toughest thing to do is trust him. God telling us no—which *is* unanswered prayer—is something we don't enjoy discussing, but it's a universal reality as Christians. So we'd be remiss if we neglected it.

In this book you will find lessons learned, exhortations given, challenges extended, and encouragements offered. I want to show you, through the lens of Scripture, how we ought to respond to God's *no*. And I want to do so, in the beginning, by taking you through two stories of unanswered prayer.

First Pregnancy

Anxiety boiled up as we pulled into the medical center's parking lot. It wasn't bad anxiety, however. It's the same feeling I had before I turned around to see my wife in her wedding dress. The anticipation was overwhelming.

Around a month prior to that day, we had found out that Shale, my wife, was pregnant. With hope-filled hearts, we stood in our bathroom eagerly awaiting the result of the pregnancy test. We had been trying so we desperately wanted to see two lines show up on the tiny screen.

And they did—barely. But barely was good enough for us. One line came up and then the other slowly, but surely, revealed itself. The test was clear: we were having a baby!

Back to the parking lot, where we were about to get a glimpse of our unborn baby for the first time via ultrasound. Shale was nine weeks along at this point. After what felt like 30 minutes trying to find a parking spot, I glanced at Shale with an antsy-but-serious smile and said, "Let's pray before we go in." I don't remember what we prayed verbatim, but it went something like this: "Heavenly Father, thank you for this day. We simply want to ask you to let this go smoothly, to let our child be healthy, growing, and nothing be wrong. But even if something is wrong, Lord, I pray you guide us through it and be our strength in the midst of it. In Jesus' name, amen."

It's not a prayer we wanted want to pray but one we needed to pray. We weren't naïve. We knew something could always be wrong—definitely with a first pregnancy.

We just didn't think it would happen to us.

The Ultrasound

Our eyes perked up when the nurse called us to go back to the ultrasound room. Swiftly and confidently, the ultrasound tech got everything ready, squirted all that goo on Shale's stomach, and we were off.

Our eyes were peeled on the monitor. *Where's the baby?* I said in my head, too nervous to ask. Since she was a mere nine weeks along, we both understood that anything we see is going to be miniscule. However, the ultrasound tech wasn't giving us great signs. After searching further, she finally said, "This [pointing to the screen] might be it, but I am not positive. We will need to send you two downstairs for a more official ultrasound."

Those are words you don't want to hear.

No Words

The second ultrasound tech was as quiet as a mouse. Other than random small talk to keep our minds off the potential tragedy of the situation, we didn't hear a peep from her. She finished the ultrasound and then advised us that we will get results soon. We just needed to wait in the lobby.

That wait was awful. We were uncertain, shaken, and afraid. We walked into the hospital with complete confidence—now that confidence was all but gone. As a nurse finally came out to give us some type of news—whether good or bad—we heard an even worse answer.

"The results are not back yet, so we will give you guys a call in a couple of days," she said.

Quickly, Shale said, "No. That's not going to work. I am not going to wait a couple days to hear if my child is okay. We will wait here. Please let us talk to somebody else."

Thankfully, they obliged. After another agonizing wait, we got the opportunity to speak with one of the head doctors in the OB department who told us one of two things was happening. One, the pregnancy was simply not far enough to detect anything yet; or two, it was a false pregnancy. We were confused by what he meant by false pregnancy, but he assured us as we left that Shale was in fact pregnant. She went from being nine weeks to six weeks along.

Though we were still shaken, we left the hospital with more confidence than we had in the waiting room.

A Second Opinion

Shale was still uneasy about the lack of communication we experienced at that visit. So was I. The only doctor who gave us any beneficial information was the one we met with last. There was no other explanation from any other doctor. As a result, we both agreed to get a second opinion.

At the time, I worked at Chick-fil-A. My phone rang at about 11 a.m. during my shift the next day. My heart skipped a beat. I knew this was it. I had fully prepared myself to hear Shale had a miscarriage. I knew the baby wasn't far along but I also knew we should've been able to see something, no matter how small.

With a distraught voice on the other end of the phone, Shale said, "Blake, the doctor said I have a blighted ovum."

"What on earth is a blighted ovum?" I responded, confused.

"He said it's when pregnancy happens but a sac is never developed," she said. "There was never a baby."

Those words hit me like a ton of bricks. They hit me like how an NFL linebacker blindsides a wide receiver running across the middle of the field. My ears were prepared to hear we lost the baby; they were not prepared, however, to hear we never had a baby. My brain had to adapt to this shocking news. *You're telling me there was never a baby?* I thought to God.

It turns out a blighted ovum is unfortunately common for first-time pregnancies. I still don't know all the biological jargon behind it, but what I did know was this: there was no baby. And though, no, we didn't have to experience the pain of a miscarriage—of a baby being conceived and then passing away—we did have to begin the process of the pain of *thinking* we had conceived a child. Of course, we had no reason not to believe there wasn't a baby. We had already taken pregnancy announcement photos.

When God Says No

After that phone call, I went straight home to Shale and we simply sat there. My mind immediately went to when I would talk to Shale's stomach as if I was talking to the baby—but I wasn't speaking to anything but Shale's stomach. That hurt. It pained me to even think about.

As time went on, we began to process it more and moved on. By the grace of God, we pushed forward.

Looking back, I realized something significant. Before we got out of the car that day, we said that prayer. We asked God to let the baby be flourishing and healthy.

But God said no to our prayer. Or, at the very least, he said "not yet."

The Second Story

Since that day, God blessed us with a beautiful little girl, Jovi Grace Long.[1] She was an entire month early, perfectly healthy. She's now three years old and wild, fun loving, and so incredibly adorable.

Piper's first night in the hospital.

Once we spent time just with Jovi, we decided to try for a second child. As soon as the doctors gave us clearance, we be-

---

[1] Since you're probably wondering in your head: Yes, she was informally named after Jon Bon Jovi, the legendary 80's music singer. I obliged just because I thought it was cute.

gan trying. To our surprise, the first day that Shale was deemed "ready" to conceive, we in fact got pregnant! And on September 5, 2021, she gave birth to our second little girl, Piper Joy Long,[2] who is the subject of this next story.

Our Second Home: The Hospital

My phone rang as I sat in my car in the parking lot at the local urgent care one afternoon. It was Shale, which I found odd. Normally she is teaching at that time, so I was immediately concerned. Dealing with a wave of unwelcomed nausea, I answered, "Hello?" with a worried tone. "Daycare just called," she explained. "Piper just projectile vomited and I'm going to get her now."

I had been going on day three or four of inconsistent-yet-uncomfortable nausea, so I was already worried about what I had—if anything. (I tested negative for everything.) Now I have Piper to worry about, which is far more concerning since she was only six weeks old at the time. Thankfully, Shale got an appointment the same day with a pediatrician at the local medical center. As I got tested for strep, flu, and Covid—and anxiously waited for the results—I also fretted about what was wrong with my youngest.

Could it be a stomach bug? Is it possible I gave her whatever I have? What if it's something worse?

A simple Google search about six-month-olds projectile vomiting doesn't do one's anxiety any good. This is why we should never go to WebMD for our symptoms. Nevertheless, there I was—nauseated and anxious for my daughter more so now because I thought it would be a good idea to Google what it could possibly be.

Since nothing was "wrong" with me, I went back to work. Shale was at the doctor with Piper trying to determine what

---

[2] Informally named after John Piper, with a nod to Christian Hedonism as her middle name is "Joy."

was wrong. Again, maybe it was a stomach bug that would go away soon—but we wanted to be safe rather than sorry. The doctor advised her vitals looked good and everything was okay, so they were sent home. As Shale put Piper in the car and called to explain the news, the first thing I heard on the phone was, "Oh, no, she just did it again! I have to go and call them back."

Something was up; this wasn't normal. Shale called the doctor and was able to go back up to the room. After further testing, Shale called me with some news.

"They want to keep her overnight," Shale said, with concern in her voice. "Just to observe her and figure out more about what's going on." Though I was upset about that news, I knew it was for the best.

Halfway through the next day we got an update. "She has a urinary tract infection," Shale said over the phone. The doctors had previously tested her urine so they knew she had a urinary tract infection (UTI). That caused them to place her on antibiotics. The bigger problem, however, is usually something causes a UTI. That's when things got worse.

Friday afternoon Shale called me to relay some information. She had good news and bad news. Good news was the doctors found an official cause: Piper had E. coli. They reason she possibly could've contracted it through birth, as Shale had E. coli while giving birth somehow. Nevertheless, now we knew how to make Piper better. They gave her more aggressive antibiotics to ensure it would work.

But that's where the bad news came in. To ensure the antibiotics would work, they wanted to keep Piper in the hospital until they were finished—which meant she'd be there a whole week. We were both upset, understandably so. But we also knew this was the wisest option. By keeping her, she would have around-the-clock care. If something went wrong, she'd be right there. For the next week, Shale and I had to juggle taking time off work to be at the hospital, and would alternate shifts. When I was at the hospital, she'd be with Jovi—and vice versa. For a week, each of us felt like a single parent. For a week, we scrambled around town to get from Point A to Point B.

A year after this trial, Shale offered thoughts of her own in her blog at: mamamusings1994.Wordpress.com, and I'd like to share them here. (There will be some overlap but I think having her perspective is important.):

"I knew something was wrong the second I saw her teacher's name pop up on my phone, calling me on Piper's third day at daycare: "She's projectile vomiting." Seeing that she was not even two months old, they got her in at the doctor almost immediately. The doctor wondered if it was just a sensitivity to her formula, so she gave us a sample of one that was soy-based, let it settle for a bit, and sent us on our way. As I was buckling Piper into the car seat, she did it again. I called and was told to come right back inside. Shortly after, I was told they wanted to admit Piper for observation. That observation quickly turned into a 9-day hospital stay when her urine came back positive for E. coli ESBL+.

Sometimes I try to convince myself it wasn't that bad, and I shouldn't have these "triggered" feelings when it comes to her hospital stay. But I do. For months after her release, any little cough, slight fever, extra fussiness, I rushed her to the doctor or worried about her like crazy. Blake did, too. Seeing these memories flooding my Facebook, the feelings of fear and sadness rush back. In the same vein, I've thought, "But it wasn't cancer. She didn't die. She got better around day 5 and only had to stay to finish off her strong antibiotics." I don't know why I try to downplay how traumatic this experience was for me as a mother. Trauma can look different for each of us.

Looking back, I truly believe this hospital stay is what triggered all of my postpartum mental health issues. Anyone who has had a sick child who required hospitalization knows how traumatic it can be. It's scary, it's lonely, it's hard. But thank goodness for a God who is there through the good and the bad, and a God who answers prayers!"

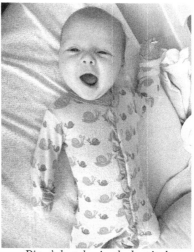

It was a crazy time. It was a trial. As she began to get sick, we both prayed continuously for it to be a simple stomach bug, but God said no. But as you read

Piper's last day in the hospital.

in Shale's blog, even amidst unanswered prayer, he still answers our prayers in other ways.

Thankfully, Piper is healthy now. In hindsight, we should have seen it coming, as she showed signs here and there that something was off. But, alas, this is how it happened. And we are grateful to God it wasn't worse—because it could've been.

God Isn't a Yes-Man

I really enjoy Jim Carrey movies. *Dumb and Dumber* is my favorite, of course. But he also starred in a movie called *Yes Man*, in which he plays Carl, a run-of-the-mill bank loan officer who just got divorced and has a gloomy outlook on life. His friend, Nick, convinces him to attend a motivational conference led by an inspirational guru.

While he is there, Terrence (the guru) singles him out because Carl (Carrey) will not agree to say *Yes!* like everybody else. Then, finally, the guru gets him to say the magic word. He essentially forces Carl to say *Yes!* to all requests, all invitations, and any opportunity that presents itself.

As the movie progresses, Carl catches up with Terrence and pleads with him to "release him from the covenant." Terrence replies by telling Carl there was never a covenant, but only opening yourself up to different possibilities.

We all know of someone like this, the character Carrey played. They say yes to *everything*. Maybe they are people-pleasers or maybe they genuinely don't know how to say no. Either way, it makes for a miserable life, as it's simply implausible to answer yes all the time.

However, God is not this way. God is not a yes-man.

God is Not a Cosmic Butler

Prosperity preachers today make God out to be some type of "yes-man." The god they speak of always says yes and never conflicts with or challenges humans' desires. In short, they make it seem like God caters to us. In this prosperity theology, God is our cosmic butler simply waiting for us to say what we want next.

This type of thinking is more prevalent within the prosperity gospel movement, and even mainstream evangelicalism is tempted to make the same error. Though most faithful Christians don't view God in light of the prosperity gospel, we can all at times succumb to it by thinking our relationship with God is transactional. Though we don't mean to, we might treat God as a divine bellhop. All we have to do is call room service (pray), ask for what we want (make our requests known to him), and he will give it to us.

Because some of us have bought into this line of thinking about God, we become disheartened and event resentful toward God when he does say no to our prayers. So we must ask this difficult question: Do we have room in our theology for God to say no to our prayers?

This Book is about God

So, Christian, do you have room in your theology for unanswered prayer? Do we understand God does, in fact, say no to many of our prayers? Even our earnest and heartfelt ones? Even the ones that sound too spiritual *not* to be answered with a resounding yes? Or do our prayers resemble more of a wish to a genie than a prayer to a sovereign God?

This book is about God. Yes, this book will cover areas of our lives and the things we go through on a day-to-day basis. We will explore real-life circumstances and will not shy away from understanding that every human responds differently to God. In the end, however, this book is about God—his character, nature, and goodness; his sovereignty, providence, and mercy toward sinners.

God wants a simple, childlike trust from his children. And he wants this trust not with blind eyes but with a believing heart.

You may close this book and understand more about your natural instincts in prayer. It may help you respond to God in better ways. That is all well and good. But I want more for you. I want more for me, even as I type these words. I want us—those who have been redeemed by the finished work of Jesus Christ—to commune with God on a deeper, more profound level. To know him more deeply, to cherish him more affectionately, to love him more wholly.

So yes, I want to reorient our minds around how God works in prayer. When we do that, we understand God more and, in turn, it will lead to a more vibrant prayer life. But in the end, I want you, the reader, to know God more. Not just intellectually, but affectionately. Not just in theory, but in practice. Not just in our minds, but in our hearts.

1

The God Who is Attentive

*God Hears, Listens, and
Inclines His Ears to our Prayers*

EVERYTHING CHANGED when I became a father. I didn't merely care for my wife and myself anymore. There was a third person in the mix—and a tiny one at that. Day by day, our little girl grew taller, weighed more, and talked clearer. She went from cooing to talking. She went from unintelligible mumbling to saying complete sentences with no confusion about what was said.

When Jovi was born, I knew she needed my utmost attention. That was my number one job outside of loving my wife: give my attention to this precious little girl that God gave us. Now that she is communicating well, she needs my attention all the more. But not only does she *need* my attention, she *wants* my attention. As a sinner, I fail many times in giving her that attention, but I know I need to clearly show Jovi that her daddy is listening, attentive, and enjoying talking with her. Whether that means I play with her, talk with her, or listen to her when she is upset. Regardless, she knows I hear her, am listening to her, and am eager to talk to her.

Our "Highest Privilege"

The same is true of our Heavenly Father, but on a much larger scale. The Bible does not talk about our prayer with God in a generic sense, but in a special way. It is not ho-hum, but intimate. It may come as a shock, but each person on earth does not have equal access to God through prayer. God has "a special place in his heart," so to speak, for his children—those who have been born again (John 3:3). Scripture is clear that not all people are God's children, but only those who have been adopted by God through the Holy Spirit (Romans 8:15-17). "The moment we are born again by the Spirit through faith in Christ (John 1:12-13; 3:5)," Tim Keller writes, "that Spirit shows us that we are not simply God's subjects but also his children, and we can converse with him as our Father (Galatians 4:5-6)."[1]

It is a special privilege to be God's child. Not everybody has that privilege. If you ask anyone in society, they will proclaim we are all God's children, but that is simply not the testimony of Scripture. The Bible teaches we are all God's creation, but only some are his children. "Adoption is the highest privilege that the gospel offers: higher even than justification," the late J.I. Packer penned. "Adoption is a family idea, conceived in terms of love, and viewing God as father. In adoption, God takes us into his family and fellowship—he establishes us as his children and heirs."[2]

Those are strong words from Packer. This book isn't about justification—being declared righteous before God—but Packer has a compelling point. He goes on: "Closeness, af-

---

[1] Timothy Keller, *Prayer: Experiencing Awe and Intimacy with God* (New York: Penguin Books, 2014), 45.

[2] J.I. Packer, *Knowing God* 20th Anniversary Edition (Downers Grove: IVP Books, 1993), 206-207.

fection and generosity are at the heart of the relationship. To be right with God the Judge is a great thing, but to be loved and cared for by God the Father is a greater."[3]

It is one thing—a miraculous thing!—to be declared righteous before God. It is another thing, according to Scripture, to be made a child of God through adoption. It is, as Packer states, our "highest privilege." Indeed, it is. Considering our former status, which we were dead in sin and trespasses (Ephesians 2:1), it is the greatest wonder in the world that God chose to make some his children.

For us to truly understand the privilege we have via our adoption—especially as it relates to prayer—let's talk through this some more before we go to prayer.

Welcome to the Family

The same day I wrote this chapter I also watched a video on Facebook that made me tear up. It was an adoption video where they recorded the court proceedings and the viewer got to see the slam of the gavel and the judge officially declare the teenager a son of the two parents.

It was beautiful to watch. The teenager went from having no family to instantly having a family. From stranger, to friend. From orphan, to son. The beauty of adoption. And here's the best part: the teenager did absolutely nothing to deserve this adoption. Do you know why he was adopted? Because the parents chose to do so. It was from the good will of their hearts to adopt that boy and change his life.

This is a wonderful picture of what happens when God saves us. But there is so much more. The teenager hadn't done things wrong and the parents didn't need to be appeased. Though there are similarities, this example—just like all examples—never paint the clearest picture of God's love for us.

---
[3] Ibid.

In our adoption, we went from enemies (Romans 5:10) to friends (John 15:15); from haters of God (Romans 1:30) to lovers of God (1 John 4:18). This is astounding. It is revolutionary, out of this world.

Our adoption into the family of God didn't merely have to have formal (heavenly) court proceedings of declaring us God's children; we had to be forgiven first. We were (and still are) sinners. It wasn't all peaches and roses beforehand. We were previously at war with God (Romans 8:7). But once he adopts us, it's over. " . . . Once we are welcomed into His family," wrote the late R.C. Sproul, "we are truly His sons and daughters, and there is no more war."[4]

We have special access to the Father as his children. We can "approach his throne of grace with boldness" (Hebrews 4:16). Boldness does not mean arrogance. Boldness, in this context, is confidence. Not confidence in ourselves, but confidence that we've been adopted into his family because of the blood of Christ. Jesus's atonement solidified our unrestricted access to the throne of grace—and we had nothing to do with it (Ephesians 2:8).

And this is why we can know for certainty that God is attentive to his children.

He Hears

God hears our prayers. I know that's one of the more elementary concepts of our faith, but it's still true. Just like needing the gospel everyday, we need to remember that God hears us each day, because we so easily forget.

Scripture has an abundance of verses indicating God's ear to our prayer:
- "For the eyes of the Lord are on the righteous, and his ears are open to their prayer" (1 Peter 3:12).

---
[4] RC Sproul, *Truths We Confess: A Systematic Exposition of the Westminster Confession of Father* (Sanford: Reformation Trust, 2019). 283.

- "The LORD is far from the wicked, but he hears the prayer of the righteous" (Proverbs 15:29).
- "When the righteous cry for help, the LORD hears and delivers them out of all their troubles" (Psalm 34:17).
- "In my distress I called upon the LORD; to my God I cried for help. From his temple he heard my voice, and my cry to him reached his ears" (Psalm 18:6)
- "But know that the LORD has set apart the godly for himself; the LORD hears when I call to him"(Psalm 4:3).

Believer, do you know God hears your prayer? Better yet, do you believe he does? Oftentimes, we know things to be true but fail to believe them in the moment. I know my wife loves me because she said her vows at our wedding, but when we're arguing I tend to forget. And that has nothing to do with her and everything to do with my heart.

The same is true with God. We know he hears us because the Bible is crystal clear in that regard. But when life gets rough, when the swim of life is upstream, when the waves crash in on us, do we believe it? Or do we resort back to trying to carry ourselves?

I imagine Christians sometimes accuse God of not hearing them—or at the very least question if he does. Either way we're in the wrong. When this happens, we have to ask ourselves this probing question: *Am I in my Bible consistently?* "We may struggle to hear his voice," Jared C. Wilson wrote, "but very often that is because the dust is so thick on our copies of his Word."[5]

The wider your Bible is open, the clearer your communication with him will be. If your Bible habitually collects dust, you won't hear a peep from the Lord. That's not because

---

[5] Jared C. Wilson, *Supernatural Power for Everyday People: Experiencing God's Extraordinary Spirit in Ordinary Life* (Nashville: Thomas Nelson, 2018), 66.

he's not hearing you or speaking to you; it's because you've stopped listening. It's as if my wife went to another country for a year and wrote letters to me everyday. I would go to the mailbox to retrieve them but never open the envelope. Yet I grumbled, whined, and threw a fit because I believed she wasn't communicating with me. The problem wasn't her, but me. I didn't take the time to open the envelope and read.

Likewise, when we keep our Bibles shut, it will become increasingly difficult to hear from God and believe he hears us. When we ask, "Is God even hearing me?" the problem is not with God's communication, but with us because we too easily neglect the book in which he speaks to us. This isn't always the case, however. Many Christians who are consistently in the Word still feel this way on occasion.

God hears you. He is there. He is "all ears." You just need to do two things. One, you need to pray. Cry out to him; go to him often—for anything. Sometimes we think he doesn't hear because . . . we're not praying. Second, open your Bible and let him speak. You may have said your prayer but you won't hear from him if your Bible is closed.

Lastly, understand that God does not merely *hear* you, but listens to you.

He Listens

One of my biggest problems in marriage is that I don't listen very well. And not listening reveals I don't care enough about what my wife is saying in that moment—and that's totally on me. But that doesn't mean I don't hear her speak. I might hear all the words she is saying but, if I'm not listening, it's going through one ear and out the other. There is a huge difference between listening and merely hearing.

God doesn't simply hear our prayers. As God's children, he also listens to our prayers. He cares about what we have to say. And unlike me, we can know for certain that God is listening to every last request, every last supplication, every last word.

Just like with hearing us, the Bible shows he listens to us in many passages.

- "We know that God does not listen to sinners. He listens to the godly person who does his will" (John 9:31 NIV).
- "Then you will call on me and come and pray to me, and I will listen to you. You will seek me and find me when you seek me with all your heart" (Jeremiah 29:12-13 NIV).
- "I cried out to him with my mouth; his praise was on my tongue. If I had cherished sin in my heart, the Lord would not have listened; but God has surely listened and has heard my prayer. Praise be to God, who has not rejected my prayer or withheld his love from me' (Psalm 66:17-20 NIV)!"[6]

As God's child, I can know he is listening to me. His ears aren't merely open; they are focused on what I am saying. That is so comforting; to know the God of the universe—the Creator and Sustainer of all things—is listening to my prayer. God listens to my prayer no matter how mumbled, how repetitive, or how messed up it is. He does not get fed up with listening, even when the prayer is saturated with sin. He doesn't ignore, even when we ask for things we know we shouldn't. He doesn't roll his eyes, even when we say one thing in our prayer and do another in practice.

Bask in that for a moment.

As God's blood-bought children, he is for us. And he thoroughly enjoys listening to our petitions. God's "listening ears" are on 24/7. Go to him.

---

[6] You might notice the different translations. I did, in fact, use those because they specifically express that God is listening. Other translations use different words but they all mean the same thing.

He Inclines

I remember the moment Jovi said her first word. No, it wasn't, "Mama" or "Dada." It was "Dundie"—our dog's name. Go figure.

Since it was her first word, she enunciated it in a way that was humorous and her eye did a funny little twitch every time she said it. Once she said her first word, from that moment we eagerly listened to every little word she said. We loved listening to her say new words and learn new things! We were attentive to her.

In the same way, God is attentive to our prayers. "Because he inclined his ear to me," Psalm 116:2 reads, "therefore I will call on him as long as I live." How amazing is this? He inclines his ear to our prayers, our calls for help!

It's not as if he merely hears our prayers.

It's not like he simply hears and listens to our prayers.

But he hears, listens, and inclines his ear to our prayers! Though all three overlap somewhat, God inclining his ear displays an eagerness to hear from us, a desire to hear from his children. There is no hesitancy, no annoyance, no distraction. God wants to hear from us. Next time you pray, imagine God leaning down and cupping his ear to hear you crystal clear. You can't nag God.

God is not in the business of ignoring his children in prayer. Go to him! Pray, pray, pray. You can rest assured that, as a child of God, he is attentive to your prayer. The Lord is eager to hear from you. He wants to listen to your pleas for help, your desire for growth, your prayers for mercy.

Setting the Foundation

This book is not merely about God being attentive to our prayers. It's about much more than that. I wanted to lay the foundation here, which is composed of two parts. First, I wanted you, the reader, to understand this book is written for children of God, those whom God has saved through the atoning death of Jesus Christ.

In a very real sense, unbelievers don't have the same privilege as Christians do. Simply put, God is not obligated to listen to the prayers of unbelievers. Tim Keller once wrote: "Sinners deserve to have their prayers go unanswered."[7]

If you are an unbeliever, I invite you to "taste and see that the Lord is good" (Psalm 34:8). Run to Christ! Collapse on him, as his arms are open to all who come to him in repentance and faith (Mark 1:15).

Second, I wanted to remind you of these precious truths before we delve into more practical circumstances. There will be times in life when we are tempted to believe God isn't there; that he's not hearing or listening to us. I hope this chapter served as a reminder. It doesn't matter if your life is collapsing or you are on top of the world. This truth still remains: God hears you, he's listening to you, and he's attentive to your prayers.

With that said, what happens when he doesn't answer our prayer? Or, we know he answers, but just not the way we'd like him to? By looking at the examples of three men in Scripture, I pray we will be able to have a biblical perspective.

---

[7] Timothy Keller, *Prayer: Experiencing Awe and Intimacy with God* (New York: Penguin Books, 2014), 237.

Prayer of Reflection:

Father, I am grateful to be able to call you Father. Not only are you my Creator, but my Father as well. You deeply love your children, and you express that love in many ways, specifically by being attentive to our prayers. You hear us, listen to us, and incline your ear to our prayer. You make it known to us that you're with us. Lord, I am thankful for your Fatherly care in my life. Help me to always remember that you are with me and hear my prayers even when my feelings say otherwise. In Jesus's name, amen.

2
Unanswered Prayer in the Bible

When God Said No to David, Paul, and Jesus

I LOVE THE BIBLE so much because it's realistic. It's not far-fetched, nor does it only talk about the good parts. It covers it all—the good and the bad, the amazing and the ugly, the great and the wicked.

And that means it's realistic about our prayer lives. It doesn't make it sound like everything always goes well. Prayer is hard, tough, and takes discipline. And yet it is the most glorious thing in the world, to be able to commune with God, our Heavenly Father. But it is also realistic about our prayers going unanswered. This is not because God is aloof, but because many times our prayers don't align with his will.

There are three prominent examples of unanswered prayer in Scripture. Indeed, there are many more than three, but I hope that the three we go over briefly will help us work from the foundation that unanswered prayer happens to the best of us—even the Son of God. Let's look at the examples of King David, the Apostle Paul, and Jesus Christ.

God Said No to David

"David begged God to spare the child" (2 Samuel 12:16 NLT). As Nathan returned home, God sent a deadly illness upon David and Bathsheba's son. And as we see in this verse, David pleaded with the Lord to keep his son alive, to spare him. For seven days, David prayed and fasted, begging the Lord to heal his son.

And then the child died (v. 19).

David was desperate, as any parent would be. He begged and cried out to the Lord. He did everything he could do to save his son. And yet, God said no. God had other plans. God was working. RC Sproul said this:

> When God said no to the pleas of David, he immediately went to church—not to whine or complain but to worship. Here we see David living *coram Deo*, before the face of God. David plead his case before the throne of the Almighty—and lost. Yet he was willing to bow before the providence of God, to let God be God.[8]

How he responded said a lot about his trust in the Lord. He wasn't whiny; he didn't throw a fit. He didn't sulk or pity himself. He said: "But now he is dead. Why should I fast? Can I bring him back again? I shall go to him," David said in verse 23, "but he will not return to me."[9] David believed his son had gone to heaven. He had confidence in God's plan, despite his prayer going unanswered. Even though he had just gone through agony over his son, he knew God had

---

[8] RC Sproul, *The Invisible Hand: Do All Things Really Work for Good?* (Phillisburg: P&R Publishing, 1996), 10.

[9] As a side note, Christians use this verse as evidence for the age or level of accountability, which teaches that children—depending on maturity level—go to heaven when they die.

better plans. In the end, David trusted God despite not receiving the outcome he so desired.

This is the exact attitude we ought to have when our prayers go unanswered. We believe God and his Word despite the results not being what we want. King David is a clear case of having the utmost confidence in the Lord even in the most excruciating of times.

Let's turn our attention to the New Testament to two more instances of unanswered prayer.

God Said No to Paul

Did you know the Apostle Paul had a vision of Heaven? In these days when one claims to see a vision of heaven via dream or near-death experience, it becomes a Hollywood movie. Not so with Paul's vision. Read his experience below.

> I must go on boasting. Though there is nothing to be gained by it, I will go on to visions and revelations of the Lord. I know a man in Christ who fourteen years ago was caught up to the third heaven—whether in the body or out of the body I do not know, God knows. And I know that this man was caught up into paradise—whether in the body or out of the body I do not know, God knows—and he heard things that cannot be told, which man may not utter. On behalf of this man I will boast, but on my own behalf I will not boast, except of my weaknesses— though if I should wish to boast, I would not be a fool, for I would be speaking the truth; but I refrain from it, so that no one may think more of me than he sees in me or hears from me. So to keep me from becoming conceited because of the surpassing greatness of the revelations, a thorn was given me in the flesh, a messenger of Satan to harass me, to keep me from becoming conceited. Three times I pleaded with the

Lord about this, that it should leave me. But he said to me, "My grace is sufficient for you, for my power is made perfect in weakness." Therefore I will boast all the more gladly of my weaknesses, so that the power of Christ may rest upon me. For the sake of Christ, then, I am content with weaknesses, insults, hardships, persecutions, and calamities. For when I am weak, then I am strong (2 Cor. 12:1-10).

All Paul said about this vision was that he was "caught up to the third heaven" (v. 2), and he "heard things that cannot be told, which man may not utter" (v. 4). This pales in comparison to the over-the-top drama of modern trips to "heaven." The Apostle Paul had an authentic, biblical vision of heaven and barely said a word about it.

But there's far more to the story. In order to keep Paul from becoming conceited about this heavenly revelation (v. 7), the Lord gave Paul "a thorn . . . in the flesh." What this thorn was, we do not truly know, but we can wonder.[10]

This thorn pained Paul so deeply that he pleaded with the Lord three times to take it away, but God didn't (v. 8). God said no to the Apostle Paul. And it wasn't even a, "No, maybe later." It was a straightforward no. Even though Paul was in pain, in discomfort, experiencing this hindrance, the Lord said no. Why? According to Paul, there was one great reason.

Paul knew, despite the Lord telling him no, everything would be fine because God's grace is sufficient. *Sufficient for what?* we may ask. Sufficient to hold us up, to keep us going, to push us forward. Sufficient for anything that may come our way in life—whether a thorn in the flesh or a fork in the road.

Do you believe God's grace is sufficient for you? What is the thorn in your flesh currently? Surely there is something,

---

[10] Some theologians speculate it was a secret struggle with sin, but others suggest it was an eye ailment, which he may have alluded to in Galatians 4:13-15.

as we all deal with various ailments to some extent. Do you trust God's grace will be sufficient to meet your needs, or is your faith crumbling from the pressure of your thorn?

God may say no to our prayers but it is never one void of grace. "... Paul's request wasn't altogether rejected," Garrett Kell wrote. "Instead of relieving pain, the Lord promised grace (2 Cor. 12:8). The thorn would deepen his dependence, increase his trust, and strengthen his reliance on the Lord; the grace would keep him from giving up on the God who said no to his prayer."[11]

But why is God's grace sufficient? Because his power is made perfect in Paul's weakness. The Lord is able to shine all the more when his children are especially weak.

When your knees are wobbly, God will hold you up.

As your heart grows faint, God will strengthen your faith.

When you simply want to give up, God will not let you go.

Like the Apostle Paul, we mustn't look at God's answer with discouragement, but opportunity. Opportunity to trust in the Lord's unwavering, unconquerable grace. Opportunity to marvel at the mercy of God. Opportunity to simply trust in the one who saved us. Paul could see God's grace in his unanswered prayer, and so should we.

God Said No to Jesus

"My Father, if it be possible, let this cup pass from me."

These words in Matthew 26:39 came from the lips of Jesus as he groaned in agony to his Father over what he was about to endure in the crucifixion. And ponder the words he uttered right before this. "My soul is very sorrowful, even to death" (v. 38). It was in this moment that we get a clear picture of the despair Jesus was feeling.

---

[11] Garrett Kell, "When God Says No to Your Earnest Prayers." The Gospel Coalition, September 24, 2020. https://www.thegospelcoalition.org/article/god-says-no-earnest-prayers/.

As Jesus finished pleading before the Father, he went back to his disciples and caught them sleeping (v. 40). He went away a second time and prayed a similar prayer: "Father, if this cannot pass unless I drink it, your will be done" (v. 42). Scripture tells us he did this one more time. Jesus prayed for the Father to remove the impending cup three times.

Jesus knew the extent of what he was about to experience. He knew he had to drink the cup.

What's the "cup"? Simply put, it's referring to the Father's wrath. Jesus wasn't about to experience mere death, as excruciating as it would be for him. He was also about to experience the full brunt of God's wrath. This knowledge compels him to pray, " . . . remove this cup from me."

Jesus understood what was about to happen to him. Of course, it was the whole reason he came—to die for our sins! And yet, staring at what was before him, he made a plea to his Father: Please remove this cup. Please find another way. Please don't do this. But he didn't let this fear—if we can call it that—overcome what he was sent to do. But the Father said no.

Then take a look at what Jesus says next. "Nevertheless," he said, "not my will, but yours, be done." That is a trust-filled prayer. That is a prayer rooted and anchored in the goodness of God. Not only because he knew the character of God—as, of course, being the second person of the Trinity—but he knew he had to endure the crucifixion to make atonement for the sins of all those who believe in him (John 3:16). If Christ quit, we are still headed for Hell. Thank God he didn't quit; thank God he trusted his Father; thank God he accomplished his mission.

It Can Happen to Us

Any rational human will be relieved to read the narrative of Jesus in the garden of Gethsemane. *It's not just me*, we say. We see Jesus showing true, human emotions. The Bible is clear that Jesus is just like us—in every respect.[12] "The Gospels reveal Christ as having the basic characteristics of humanity," RC Sproul wrote. "He walks, He talks, He becomes tired, He eats, He drinks, He cries, He manifests every human emotion and every dimension of the physical aspect of mankind (see, for example, Matt. 8:24; Luke 7:34; John 11:35)."[13] Jesus was—and still is—God in the flesh. We love to emphasize the God part, as we should. It's imperative for one to believe in the "Godness" of Jesus. If Jesus wasn't God then he couldn't die for us nor live for us. But how often do we meditate on the humanity of Jesus? We should receive just as much comfort from Jesus's humanity as his deity, because, at the most fundamental level, Jesus knows what we're going through.

Jesus knows our pain because he experienced the worst of it.

Jesus knows our tears because he wept over Lazarus (John 11:35).

Jesus knows our heartache because he felt that on the cross when God laid his wrath upon him.

And Jesus knows our struggles with unanswered prayer because, as we saw in the garden, his Father said no to him just as he says no to us sometimes. If it happened to Christ, it will happen to us. If the Father denied Jesus's plea to remove the cup, then we should brace ourselves for when he denies our plea for deliverance. Denying our pleas doesn't mean God has abandoned us; it means he is using that particular pain, heartache, or struggle to mold us more into the image of his Son (Romans 8:28-29). It means he is using our struggle to make us stronger in him.

---

[12] It's vital to understand that though Jesus was like us in every respect as Hebrew 4:15 states, it doesn't mean he also had a sin nature. He was, and is, as human as we are—yet without sin!

[13] R.C. Sproul. "Perfectly Human." TableTalk Magazine, December 2015.

Your Will be Done

At the end of Jesus's plea before God, he says, "Your will be done." Again, that is a prayer of trust, a prayer of unwavering commitment to God's mission. Jesus knew his mission—to die for sinners like you and me. And for a moment in the garden—overcome with pure, unrelenting agony—Jesus asked the Father to remove the cup. Jesus was asking to take a detour.

But as we know—and as Jesus knew—there wasn't a detour. Jesus came to seek and save the lost (Luke 19:10), and he had to complete that beautiful, righteous work by dying on the "old, rugged cross" as the old hymn says. With that in mind, he submitted to the Father. "Your will be done," Jesus said. In the end, his will aligned with the Father's will. It always did, it always has, it always will. We must learn a valuable lesson from the example of Jesus.

When was the last time we prayed, "Your will be done" in a specific situation? I am not talking about reciting the Lord's Prayer before our day or a meal. I am talking about praying when something is happening in our life that is simply wrecking us emotionally, physically, and spiritually. When we ask God to take away the pain but it keeps persisting—what is our response? When we plead for God to remove the pain yet it abides—what do we do? Not only did he not take it away, but it also got worse. God said no; not yet, not now. In the midst of unending pain and anguish, do we look to Christ's example in the garden and say, "Your will be done," or do we become bitter and scream, "Why won't you listen to me?"

Let us not become faint of heart, for God will never forsake us (Deut. 31:6). May we not grow bitter or anxious, for God cares for us (1 Pet. 5:7). Let us never say, "God, you just don't understand my pain. You don't understand what I'm going through."

Have you ever said that? Have those words—or something similar—ever left your lips? Have you thought them? If so, I encourage you to repent. God *does* understand our pain—all of our pain. He understands our pain better than we do. The Lord understands what we're going through. He went through worse for us. Our response to unanswered prayer shouldn't be numbness, but trust. It shouldn't be bitterness, but hopefulness. Trust that God is working everything together for our good (Romans 8:28). Hope that one day, "there will be no more death, sadness, crying, or pain. All the old ways are gone" (Revelation 21:4). We have to experience the "old ways" for a moment, but glory is coming soon.

Psalm 88

These stories of unanswered prayer show us things sometimes get darker before they get brighter. Is your faith prepared for that?

Psalm 88 is depressing. It's the only psalm that ends with darkness, not hope. No praise comes at the conclusion but only more pain and confusion. What are we to make of this? I believe this psalm is a great example of what we go through when it seems as though God has turned away, that he has not answered our prayer and has left us for ourselves.

Before we dive further, go ahead and read it.

O Lord, God of my salvation, I cry out day and night before you. Let my prayer come before you; incline your ear to my cry! For my soul is full of troubles, and my life draws near to Sheol. I am counted among those who go down to the pit; I am a man who has no strength, like one set loose among the dead, like the slain that lie in the grave, like those whom you remember no more, for they are cut off from your hand. You have put me in the depths of the pit, in the regions dark and deep. Your wrath lies heavy upon me, and you overwhelm me with all your waves. You have caused my companions to shun me; you have made me a horror to them. I am shut in so that I cannot escape; my eye grows dim through sorrow. Every day I call upon you, O Lord; I spread out my hands to you. Do you work wonders for the dead? Do the departed rise up to praise you? Is your steadfast love declared in the grave, or your faithfulness in Abaddon? Are your wonders known in the darkness, or your righteousness in the land of forgetfulness? But I, O Lord, cry to you; in the morning my prayer comes before you. O Lord, why do you cast my soul away? Why do you hide your face from me? Afflicted and close to death from my youth up, I suffer your terrors; I am helpless. Your wrath has swept over me; your dreadful assaults destroy me. They surround me like a flood all day long; they close in on me together. You have caused my beloved and my friend to shun me; my companions have become darkness.

How many times have you cried out to God all day and night but it seems like he's not listening? How many moments has your soul felt "full of troubles?" How many days has it felt as if God is simply ignoring you?

Even amidst a psalm that ends in a low note, there is still a vast amount of grace embedded within. It looks forward to what is to come. When it feels like wrath is falling down on us, we can know for certain that Christ has come. When it appears that God is hiding his face from us, we remember the cross and know that God has set his divine affection on us. He is not hidden. He is near and in plain sight, ready for us to keep coming back to him in prayer.

God is Doing Something

God doesn't say no for its own sake. He's not some power-hungry CEO that takes enjoyment out of rejecting requests. It's not as if he gets a thrill out of not answering the prayers of his children. When God says no, it's for a reason.

We may never get to know that reason, and thankfully we don't need to. But we must remind ourselves that God has a reason for everything, especially when he leaves prayers unanswered. When we think God is aloof, just minding his own business and not paying a lick of attention to us; when we wonder if God even knows we're talking; when it seems like he is turning his back on us—it's in those moments of pain, of heartache, of confusion that God is working. He is always working. "God is always doing 10,000 things in your life," John Piper tweeted, "and you may be aware of three of them."[14]

Don't think for one second that God has stopped caring, stopped loving, and stopped providing for you. When you lose your job and your financial stability flies out the window, remember that not one sparrow falls to the ground apart from our Father. If he cares enough for the sparrow, he certainly will care more for you, his beloved child. When your child just died unexpectedly, remember that the Father killed his own son (Is. 53:10)—so that you may reap what Christ sowed on earth.

No matter what happens in our lives—no matter what prayer goes unanswered—we can rest assured that God is with us. He's doing something. And many times we don't see what he's doing until years later. If God wants us to see what he's up to, he will show us. Outside of that, he simply wants our childlike trust and obedience. He wants us to understand that his denial of our prayer is not proof of his hatred of us, but his love for us. As kids, when we asked our parents for something repeatedly and they said no each time, we got upset. We didn't truly understand why. But parents see the bigger picture. They are more mature. They have experienced

---

[14] Desiring God, "Piper: 'God is always doing 10,000 things in your life, and you may be aware of 3 of them.'" *Twitter*. November 8, 2012. https://twitter.com/desiringgod/status/266584993881550849

more life. They know what we're asking for will wind up hurting us, even though we don't know it yet.

God is omniscient, which means he knows all things. Many times he denies our prayers because he knows it will bring stress to our lives. It will shake us up; it will bring more suffering. We don't see it, so we complain. But God will not withhold anything that is for our good. If our prayer goes unanswered, we must trust that God didn't want that for us—even if our prayer was for something good.

But those times when the world is crumbling around us and things only seem to be getting worse, how do we pray? I believe, if we are faithful to Scripture, we have to pray these words:

"Even if you don't."

Prayer of Reflection

Heavenly Father, it's evident in your Word that you don't answer all of our prayers. Help me be okay with that. Help me believe that it's a good thing you tell us no sometimes. You didn't answer the prayer of King David, the Apostle Paul—you didn't even answer your beloved Son's prayer in the garden. Lord, give me the grace to believe that behind every "no," is your steadfast love. Thank you for unanswered prayer. In Jesus's name, amen.

3

Lord, I Trust You

Responding with Unwavering Trust

REWIND WITH ME back to the introduction. There I told you about our experience with unanswered prayer. I wrote briefly about the prayer before we walked into the hospital. At the end of it we said, "But even if something is wrong." Though that was not something we wanted to pray or enjoyed thinking about, we knew we ought to pray it because we knew things don't always go according to plan.

In this chapter I want to focus on that sentence—"even if you don't." This sentence is inextricably linked to our trust, our belief, our confidence in the Lord. But what does this mean practically? How does it look? I think to take a deeper look we must turn our attention to a familiar Old Testament story featuring three men.

The Fiery Furnace

King Nebuchadnezzar had just made a golden image for everybody to bow down and worship. His rule was if you didn't worship the golden image, you would be thrown into the fiery furnace.

Shadrach, Meschasch, and Abednego decided to take a stand as true worshippers of God to not bow the knee to this golden image:

> And whoever does not fall down and worship shall be cast into a burning fiery furnace. There are certain Jews whom you have appointed over the affairs of the province of Babylon: Shadrach, Meshach, and Abednego. These men, O king, pay no attention to you; they do not serve your gods or worship the golden image that you have set up." Then Nebuchadnezzar in furious rage commanded that Shadrach, Meshach, and Abednego be brought. So they brought these men before the king. Nebuchadnezzar answered and said to them, "Is it true, O Shadrach, Meshach, and Abednego, that you do not serve my gods or worship the golden image that I have set up? Now if you are ready when you hear the sound of the horn, pipe, lyre, trigon, harp, bagpipe, and every kind of music, to fall down and worship the image that I have made, well and good. But if you do not worship, you shall immediately be cast into a burning fiery furnace. And who is the god who will deliver you out of my hands?" Shadrach, Meshach, and Abednego answered and said to the king, "O Nebuchadnezzar, we have no need to answer you in this matter. If this be so, our God whom we serve is able to deliver us from the burning fiery furnace, and he will deliver us out of your hand, O king. But if not, be it known to you, O king, that we will not serve your gods or worship the golden image that you have set up." (Daniel 3:11-18)

These three men displayed courageous faith, fearless determination, and unshakeable confidence in the Lord. And it wasn't because they were so amazing, but because they knew, above all else, that God was with them. God was greater than King Nebuchadnezzar.

Notice at the end of this passage, the three men proclaim, "But if not, be it known to you O king, that we will not serve your gods or worship the golden image that you have set up" (v. 18). In the verse earlier they mention the God they served—the one true God!—will deliver them from the fiery flames of the furnace. And yet they say, "But if not." They have the utmost confidence that God can and will deliver them from the furnace, but they will still not bow the knee if he chooses not to. They will not compromise.

The unshakeable confidence we witness in these three men is certainly worthy of emulation. It's the response we should have when thrown in our own fiery furnace, metaphorical or not. We want to believe, just like they did, that God is still good and faithful even if he doesn't answer our prayer the way we desire. We want to be able to say, "But if not," just like these men.

We do the opposite, however. We may even say the words with our lips but our actions and thoughts say otherwise. We profess to trust God even if he says no, but when rubber meets the road, that trust is tossed out the window. We go from trusting to doubting, from confidence in the Lord to confidence in self, from undying faith to ever-faltering faith. We just can't get it together.

Why does this happen? Why is it that, for many of us, our faith seems to wobble more when God doesn't answer our prayer? I can think of at least two reasons and one is more likely than the other.

Reasons for the Struggle

We believe in a quasi-prosperity theology. We know the prosperity gospel nonsense of our day and in decades past.

From Creflo Dollar to Kenneth Copeland, the prosperity theology mumbo-jumbo abounds. We know good and well to steer clear of that. The problem, however, is what author and pastor Dean Inserra called the "new prosperity gospel."

Disciples of the new prosperity gospel are seeking something experiential and lasting, but we must realize that they don't need to go around the gospel to find what they are looking for in their lives. God's love, in Christ, is the experience.[15]

This creeps in unnoticed because it looks good on paper; however, in practice it reeks of prosperity gospel garbage. It makes us the focus, not God. Though it's not as overt as the prosperity gospel of Kenneth Copeland, this theology is perfectly fine with making Jesus the center—we just want to be there with him. If we aren't careful, any well-meaning Christian could fall prey to this. We must be discerning, cautious, and focused on the truth. Believing in it has a direct correlation with how we respond when God doesn't answer our prayers.

If we are tempted to believe in this theology, we might believe God is obligated to answer our prayers. That simply couldn't be further from the truth, as "[God] does as he pleases" (Ps. 115:3). In this movement, there is truth but it's sprinkled with just enough heresy that it spoils the entire message. One drop of poison does the job. Though God is always eager to hear from his children, he is not under any obligation to answer *all* our prayers.

We are spiritually immature. We are all immature to some extent because we don't have glorified bodies yet. However, some might make a habit out of believing God will always say yes even when the Bible is clear that he doesn't.

---

[15] Dean Inserra, *Getting Over Yourself: Trading Believe-In-Yourself Religion for Christ-Centered Christianity* (Chicago: Moody Publishers, 2021) 84.

Here are some diagnostic questions to see if you're spiritually immature:
- Do you doubt God's goodness when your prayer goes unanswered?
- Do you respond by sulking or thinking you've done something wrong?
- Do you wonder if God doesn't care for you anymore?

If you answered yes to any of those, it might be a sign that you are spiritually immature. How, then, do we fix this immaturity? The answer is not looking inward, but outward. Not staring at ourselves, but fixating our eyes on Jesus. And we must do this by studying God's Word. If we aren't saturating ourselves with Scripture, we will not make progress in our walk with Christ. We need to grow more in holiness, more in the image of his son. The more we grow in holiness, the easier it will be to say, "Even if you don't."

And that is the goal. We want to be able to confidently say, "Even if you don't."

"Lord, please heal my body of this cancer, *but even if you don't*, I still trust you."

"God, please keep us safe on our road trip, *but even if you don't*, you're still good."

"Father, please give me this promotion I've been seeking for months, *but even if you don't*, I know your plan is best."

World is Crashing Down

"Sometimes when God closes a door," Jared C. Wilson tweeted, "he doesn't open a window."[16] In this tweet Wilson was dismantling the popular phrase, "When God closes a door, he opens a window." Though that analogy could be true sometimes, it's not valid every time and could be dan-

---
[16] Jared C. Wilson, "Sometimes when God closes a door, he doesn't open a window. He wants you inside when the building collapses. The question: Will Christ be enough?" *Twitter*. July 8, 2017.

gerous to some who may think God will always give a way out of something. We must reject this idea, as it can give Christians the false impression that God always creates an escape.

Wilson went on. "He wants you inside when the building collapses. The question: Will Christ be enough?"[17] Being inside when the building collapses is the epitome of "Even if you don't." Even if God leaves us inside, do we believe he is good? Just because it was destroyed doesn't mean God has ceased loving us or that he has been dethroned. We're still in it for a reason.

Ultimately, what this comes down to is the question Wilson asks in his tweet. *Is Christ enough for you?*

Is Christ enough when you can't seem to find a job that supports your family? Is Christ enough when it feels like everybody is out to get you? Is Christ enough when a loved one died unexpectedly? Is Christ enough when you are on your deathbed?

Jesus should be enough for us. Our goal should be able to say this: "Even if you don't rescue me from this trial, I still trust you."

His Love Behind the "No"

The beauty of trusting the Lord enough to say, "Even if you don't" is that it reveals we have assurance of his love. Do you have assurance of God's love for you?

How many times growing up did your parents say no to you, yet you never lacked assurance of their love? You knew they loved you even when their answer didn't feel great. You may have disliked their answer and wondered why they didn't say yes, but you didn't doubt their love for you.

As a parent now for three years, I completely understand

---
[17] Ibid.

this. I tell my daughter no many times each day—partly because it's the responsible thing to do when she gets too close to the stove—and I do so out of love. My "no" isn't proof of the absence of my love for her, but is an expression of it.

The same is true with our Heavenly Father, but to a much greater extent. Not everybody has great parents. Many have parents who are unloving, deadbeat, and couldn't care less. This is not so with God. God is not a deadbeat, but a Heavenly Father who is always there, always caring, always loving—even when he says no. God tells us no to stretch our faith, to point us to something bigger. Oftentimes God's "no" simply means he wants us to rest satisfied in him.

Prayer of Reflection

Lord, I trust you. Unfortunately my actions—in many times and places—reveal that is untrue about my heart. Too many situations make evident that my trust is not in you, but myself. But Lord, at the end of the day, I trust you. I trust you with my life, my salvation, my very soul. When life is easy, I trust you; when life is hard, I trust you. Help me, by your Spirit, to carry that out—for you are infinitely worthy of my trust. In Jesus's name, amen.

4

Lord, All I Need is You

Responding with Contentment

IN 2005, TOM BRADY—legendary NFL quarterback and arguably the greatest quarterback of all time—did an interview with *60 Minutes*. This interview went viral—and still remains popular because of what he said. "Man, I'm making more money now than I thought I could ever make playing football," Brady explained. "Why do I have three[18] Super Bowl rings and still think there is something greater out there for me? ... It's got to be more than this."

Tom Brady—a person who seems to have everything the world has to offer—is still chasing contentment. After all this success, he is left feeling unsatisfied.

Christians read this story and perk up. We know why he's not satisfied. We know why he's still pursuing contentment. Brady certainly doesn't profess to be a follower of Jesus. In other words, Brady doesn't have Christ. Anybody outside of

---
[18] The crazy thing is now Brady has seven Super Bowl rings.

Christ will not have final contentment, but will perpetually be chasing the winds of contentment.

Abiding contentment is possible for those in Christ. The Apostle Paul makes that clear in his letter to the Philippian church:

> Not that I am speaking of being in need, for I have learned in whatever situation I am to be content. I know how to be brought low, and I know how to abound. In any and every circumstance, I have learned the secret of facing plenty and hunger, abundance and need. I can do all things through him who strengthens me. (Philippians 4:11-13)

And yet, Christians continue to struggle with being satisfied in life. Whether it's a job, finances, relationships, or something else, we seem to be as discontent as the next man.

In this chapter, I want to discuss how we ought to respond to unanswered prayer with contentment. In order to get there, though, I want to talk about some of the passages that seem to indicate that God will give us anything we ask for. My plan is not to spend an exorbitant amount of time on each one, but simply to show the true meaning of the passage. We're going to discuss Matthew 7:7-11, John 16:23, and Psalm 37:4.

Ask and You Shall Receive

> Ask, and it will be given to you; seek, and you will find; knock, and it will be opened to you. For everyone who asks receives, and the one who seeks finds, and to the one who knocks it will be opened. Or which one of you, if his son asks him for bread, will give him a stone? Or if he asks for a fish, will give him a serpent? If you then, who are evil, know how to give good gifts to your children, how much more

will your Father who is in heaven give good things to those who ask him! (Matt. 7:7-11)

On its face, this verse seems to imply that God will give us whatever we desire simply if we ask. But if we continue looking at the following verses, we will see that is not what it is saying.

Jesus is referring to our needs rather than our wants in this passage, as he uses the analogy of a father giving his son what he needs. This passage is not saying God will give us what we want, but what we need. Our Father will give us what we need if we just ask him. But he may not always give us what we want—and that's a good thing. Many times what we desire will ruin us, discourage us, and frustrate us in the end.

God, as our sovereign, good, holy Father, reserves the right to distinguish between what we want and need. But we shouldn't think he is abandoning us if he doesn't answer our wishes.

Indeed, this is fundamentally what happens in unanswered prayer. God says no and we become discontent, when the opposite response should be true of us. We get discouraged, sulk, and act as if God doesn't love us because we don't understand that he doesn't always give us what we want, but only what we need. This is when we have the opportunity to be truly content with what we have. Understanding that God always gives us what we need should calm our hearts to the point of pure contentment.

In Jesus' Name

In that day you will ask nothing of me. Truly, truly, I say to you, whatever you ask of the Father in my name, he will give it to you. (John 16:23)

This verse is of utmost important because it has so many implications. In this text we are told that, if we ask anything of the Father in Jesus' name, he will give it to us (v. 23). What does this mean, then? If we throw "In Jesus' name" onto the end of every prayer, does that mean the Father will automatically say yes to them? Once again, we know the answer is no from experience, but why does this text make it sound like the opposite?

It comes down to truly understanding what it means to pray in Jesus' name. To pray in Jesus' name is not some magical incantation or a religious chant we must use at the end of every prayer; there is no inherent power in that phrase that will cause us to get what we desire. We can't say, "Father, give me a nice house, lots of money, and fame—in Jesus' name," and expect to get that. It's not as if it's our secret weapon and all we have to do is recite it. To believe that is to believe Jesus is more akin to a genie than he is God in the flesh.

What, then, does it mean to pray in the name of Jesus? What significance does it truly have for our prayer lives? To pray in Jesus' name is a humble affirmation of our complete dependence on the merits of Christ as the only way to commune with the Father. When we pray in Jesus' name, we acknowledge we can't get to the Father but by Jesus Christ (John 14:6). If Jesus didn't live for us, die in our place, resurrect, and ascend to the Father's right hand, then we don't have special access to him. But Jesus opened a way for us and our prayers through his work!

Therefore, when we pray and say *in Jesus' name*, let us not believe it's the magic formula that will always cause God to answer our prayers; rather, let us remember that we pray in the name of Jesus because he's the only way we get to God. And when God says no to our prayers, we can be content because we have Christ.

Delight Yourself in the Lord

> Delight yourself in the LORD, and he will give you the desires of your heart. (Psalm 37:4)

Back in 2015, Oprah appeared on *The Late Show* with Stephen Colbert and they both spoke for a bit about their favorite Bible passage. Oprah explained that her favorite verse was Psalm 37:4, which reads: "Delight yourself in the LORD, and he will give you the desires of your heart." When we understand this verse correctly, it's a thing of beauty.

Unfortunately, Oprah missed it. She said, "Lord has a wide range: compassion, love, forgiveness, kindness. So you delight yourself in those virtues where the character of the Lord is revealed." From the very beginning she is detaching God from the verse, and simply using generic virtues we all can achieve.

She went on: "So you delight yourself in those virtues, where the character of the LORD is revealed. Delight thyself in goodness, delight thyself in kindness, and you will receive the desires of your heart. If you focus on being a force for good, then goodness will come."

There's one problem with all of this: that's not at all what the verse means. Psalm 37:4 doesn't mean we will receive the pleasures and desires of our hearts if we desire good qualities like goodness and kindness.

Here's what this verse means: the moment we delight our hearts in God is the moment he will cause our desires to align with his will. Does this mean we're never to pray for our desires (because sometimes our desires aren't that holy)? Of course not. "We are indeed to ask God to fulfill desires—let's not shrink back from that," Tim Keller wrote. "The Psalms are filled with examples of worshippers pouring out their hearts' desires to God."[19]

There is nothing wrong with praying for God to grant the desires of our hearts. That is natural. God wants us to pray for that, but he wants our desires to align with his desire for our life. We can't say we delight in the Lord, pray for

---

[19] Timothy Keller, *Prayer: Experiencing Awe and Intimacy with God* (New York: Penguin Books, 2014), 226.

whatever we want, and then expect to receive it. That's lip service. This is because we're not truly delighting ourselves in the Lord. But when this does happen correctly, it's beautiful and we should be in awe of God.

When God Says No

Do you know of any parents that never say no to their child? I think we can all name a few. The habit of always saying yes to your children will wind up being awful for them in the future. Not only does it cause them to feel entitled to everything, but also they will possibly grow up in that entitlement and believe everything ought to be handed to them.

Of course, this is not so with God. He does say no to his children. If you're a parent like I am, it is good to say no. Your child(ren) may hate it right now, but one day they will understand. The same is true for us as God's children. We may not like that he says no to us, but if we understand God's love for us, we will be okay with unanswered prayer. We can be secure in God's delight over us, even as he says no. It is good to believe this. In contrast, believing he will give us anything we ask only sets us up for spiritual failure. We become bitter when he says no and resort to abandoning our trust in him.

When God says no, we must learn to be content, regardless of the situation we're in. When God says no to our prayer—even our earnest prayer—contentment should leak out, not resentment or bitterness.

Godliness with Contentment

But godliness with contentment is great gain, for we brought nothing into the world, and we cannot take anything out of the world. But if we have food and clothing, with these we will be content. But those who desire to be rich fall into temptation, into a snare, into many senseless and harmful desires that plunge people into ruin and destruction. For the love of money is a root of all kinds of evils. It is through this craving that some have wandered away from the faith and pierced themselves with many pangs. (1 Timothy 6:6—10)

To be content is to be satisfied with and in God. In a day and age when discontentment runs amuck, Christians can truly stand out by simply being content. We struggle with contentment, though. We're not content with our finances—if only I had more money, then I could buy our dream home. We're not content with our occupation—if only I worked there then we wouldn't have any worries. We're not content with our church—if only my church had a better children's ministry then we'd be happy.

Lurking around every nook and cranny is the sinful attitude of discontentment. We champion that we are "in the world, but not of the world." Yet when it comes to contentment, we behave just like the world. We need the power of the Holy Spirit—God himself—to be truly content. First Timothy explains the reasoning why we should be content. " . . . for we brought nothing into the world, and we cannot take anything out of the world." We were born with nothing and we will die with nothing—so why do we complain of not having things? Godliness with contentment is a great gain.

Contentment in a discontent world makes people turn their heads. It makes us stand out when the norm is to complain. But so many times we are discontent because God says no to our prayers. But just as contentment reveals our satisfaction with God, our discontentment showcases our dissatisfaction with him.

In a culture of discontentment, complaining, and murmuring, God calls us to contentment, to satisfaction, to being happy with where God has us. And why can we be content? Because we have God.

Whatever the Situation

Not that I am speaking of being in need, for I have learned in whatever situation I am to be content." (Philippians 4:11)

What is your situation? Are you struggling to make end's meet? Is your weight not where you want it to be? Do you find yourself continually wanting a new vehicle? God is calling you to contentment regardless of your situation. To be satisfied in him. To be fulfilled with what God has given you.

In the above passage, the Apostle Paul is talking about his time in prison, which is where he wrote Philippians. He continues: "I know how to be brought low, and I know how to abound. In any and every circumstance, I have learned the secret of facing plenty and hunger, abundance and need. I can do all things through him who strengthens me" (vv. 12—13). The last verse, of course, is quite possibly the most famous verse in the Bible. And it is simultaneously the most misinterpreted verse. It is not referring to throwing touchdowns, dunking basketballs, or acing your big science exam. No, Paul is referring to his contentment in Christ.

He had gone through every situation we could think of. He experienced little, he experienced a lot, but in every situation he learned to be content with what he had. He knew he could do all things—be content in whatever circumstance—because Christ is his strength.

Are we content in every situation? I know it's difficult to be content because we still reside in our body of flesh, but are we really content? This ultimately comes down to our satisfaction with God himself. Do we believe he is taking care of us? Do we affirm his sovereign care over our lives, specifically as his children? He knows the number of hairs upon our head (Luke 12:7); he cares for the birds of the field, so we know he cares much more for us (Matthew 6:26). With all of this in mind, how can we *not* be content in every situation?

Believer, God has placed you in the situation you are in. The job you have was given to you by God. Your finances ultimately belong to him. Your vehicle, though it may be on the verge of catastrophe, was given to you by God.

When we understand that God is caring for us—and truly believe it—then contentment is easy whether it's with a little or a lot. That's why, therefore, we can be content with unanswered prayer because we know, above all else, that God cares for us and will provide what we need.

Seek First His Kingdom

But seek first the kingdom of God and his righteousness, and all these things will be added to you." (Matthew 6:33)

This passage in Matthew—including the preceding verses—is the juggernaut for how we become content as Christians. In the preceding verses, Jesus explains that believers are totally and completely taken care of by their Heavenly Father. In verse 25, Jesus exhorts us not to be anxious about anything. Why? Because if we know our Father takes care of the birds, then he will certainly take care of his blood-bought children (v. 26). And how do we know that? Because Jesus tells us we're far more valuable than birds (v. 26b).

When this passage refers to anxiety, it is not talking about clinical anxiety, but sinful anxiety.[20] The command not to be anxious is simply that: a command. If we become anxious, that means we are sinning against God because we are not truly trusting in his divine provision. Along with anxiety comes our need for control, which leads to

---

[20] Though there is much debate around the topic of clinical or chemical anxiety, I do believe Scripture gives evidence, through the fall of man, that people—including Christians—can genuinely suffer from this type of anxiety, which in itself is not sinful.

discontentment. Anxiety and discontentment are directly linked. When we rest in the providence of God, it's far easier to be content with our situation. Ultimately, it comes down to this. When we seek the kingdom of God first before anything else, we will have that assurance of being cared for, which will give birth to contentment. Seeking the kingdom of God and his righteousness rids us of any discontentment that may swell up in our hearts. In the end, our contentment comes down to how much we're trusting in the sovereignty of God. "Contentment," Don Currin once said, "is an embracing of the sovereignty of God; working all things after the counsel of his will and not ours."[21]

Currin gets right to the point. Whether or not we are content comes down to us trusting in the sovereignty of God over our lives. Do we believe he is in control, or do we believe we are in control? The former leads to supernatural contentment; the latter leads to potentially destructive sin.

Let's get right to the heart: when God says no to our prayers, we can remain content because we know that he cares for us. His "no" is not a sign of anger or annoyance, but of love and care.

Will God give us anything we ask for? The answer is an obvious no. But when we are fixated on the sovereignty of God and content with what he has given us, hearing him say no doesn't frustrate us like it could if we doubted his character.

Part of the problem with our frustration to unanswered prayer might come down to us. Are we doing something wrong?

---

[21] Don Currin. (2021, December 6). *Contentment is an embracing of the sovereignty of God; working all things after the counsel of his will and not ours.* [Status update]. Facebook. https://www.facebook.com/profile.php?id=100007533195852

Prayer of Reflection

Father, give me a content heart. So many times, and in so many different ways, I find myself not being content with what you've given me. Please forgive me. Help me be content with my life. Help me have contentment in my work, my marriage, my finances, my *everything*. I believe you are enough; help me live like it. In Jesus's name, amen.

5
Lord, Forgive Me

Responding with Repentance

A WHILE BACK THERE was a pastoral vacancy in my town. In my mind it was the perfect opportunity. I noticed one day the former pastor was moving and thought to myself, "God, are you doing something here?" As I thought about it, I decided it just wasn't the right time. I didn't think I was ready.

But then my wife brought it up the next day. I took that as a sign God leaving the door ajar. I thought, "If my wife is on board with this, then maybe God is telling me this is something I should pursue."

With that, we began to pray—and pray a lot. Never in my life have I prayed for something so much. My mind was fixated on the prospect of officially beginning pastoral ministry, and most certainly doing so in my local area. The more I prayed, the more I felt God opening the door. To make a long story short, I was wrong. The door was technically unlocked, but I think I pushed it open by force. Safe to say, the position didn't work out. I withdrew my name before they called a new pastor there.

In hindsight, I see the amount of sin that was hidden within my prayers. *Blake,* you might ask, *are you really saying we can sin when we pray?*

Absolutely.

How Do We Sin in Prayer?

If we believe sin is not merely something we do, but who we are, then it's fair to conclude that we sin in our prayers. We may not do it with every prayer, but it likely shows up more often than not. Sin can creep up in the oddest places—even prayer—if we're not paying attention.

So how do we sin in prayer? How can something so holy, so reverent, so godly like communing with God be soaked in sin? At the foundation, it's possible because we are still sinners. Let's talk about a few ways we sin in prayer.

Wrong Motives

"You ask and do not receive," James, the half-brother of Jesus, says in James 4:3, "because you ask wrongly, to spend it on your passions." The primary way we sin in prayer is due to impure or sinful motives. Our motives are drenched in selfishness. And this verse tells us this is directly linked with unanswered prayer. In other words, James says God doesn't answer our prayers when they are bathed in unholy motives. We do this habitually and are unaware of it until we reflect on why our prayer went unanswered. We don't see it in the moment because we are too wrapped up in what we want.

Kevin Halloran, author of *When Prayer is a Struggle: A Practical Guide for Overcoming Obstacles in Prayer*, mentions the issue of impure motives in prayer by saying:

> When we're looking at the sinful motives behind our prayers, we need to look at their root causes. James

mentions several sins that lie behind wrong motives: bitter jealousy, selfish ambition, covetousness, and disorder. We could express any of these sins by asking for something with wrong motives or for selfish reasons—such as a Ferrari or a winning lottery ticket. We can even ask for something that is seemingly good with the wrong motives, such as relational blessings or a bigger ministry.[22]

My selfish ambition, for example, showed up when praying for the pastoral position I mentioned previously. It was like a Scooby Doo episode—the villain turned out to be my own sin. I thought I had good motives, but in hindsight, I didn't. I deceived myself. Part of me desired the position because I do truly want to be a pastor. I want to shepherd a flock, preach the Word, counsel his sheep, etc. But part of me also wanted the position for the title and the sense of pride I would feel being a pastor. I was dishonest with myself and dishonest with God. I wanted it so badly that I had put blinders up. I wasn't surprised to finally feel compelled to withdraw my name, as I could feel the divine tug on my heart to get over myself.

We've all done this. We've all prayed for something to happen because it would benefit us. Imagine you're up for a promotion at work. You pray tirelessly for God to give you the promotion so you can provide more for your family. Not only that, you can give more things to your children they've never had. Now they can have those nice pair of shoes or the next Xbox (or whatever kids are playing these days). Those are great things. However, in the deep recesses of your heart, you may care about those things, but they aren't king of your heart—you are. You don't ultimately want the promotion to provide more for your family, but the satisfaction and pride

---

[22] Kevin Halloran, *When Prayer is a Struggle: A Practical Guide for Overcoming Obstacles in Prayer* (Phillipsburg: P&R Publishing Company, 2021), 74.

you feel with bearing the title. And, of course, more money is never a bad thing in your book.

Then the heartbreak comes. Your buddy Steve got picked for the promotion over you. But he's not really your buddy—not anymore, at least. You despise him now. You start to see all his flaws. And now you're upset with the Lord because he didn't give you what you thought was rightfully yours. You worked hard *and* did massive amounts of overtime. Your boss should've picked you. God should've given you the promotion. But he didn't. He said no to your prayers.

Put yourself in this scenario. You can respond in many ways, but let's boil it down to two.

Response #1: ***Anger***. You become bitter with God because you felt entitled to the promotion. *Why wouldn't he give me something that would benefit my family?* It almost seems cruel. You begin to harden your heart toward God and now your relationship with him that was once like a spiritual teeter-totter is now broken and you're stuck at the bottom. The more you think about it, the angrier you get at God.

Response #2: ***Repentance***. Upon reflecting on this unanswered prayer, you come to realize why God didn't answer. Think about what would've happened if he had said yes. Would your wife and children have more things? Yes. A bigger house, a newer car that didn't break down constantly, and that cool Xbox the kids have been wanting. Your financial life would have been a breeze. But the promotion gives birth to a bigger problem in your life. Now that you received a promotion, you feel as though you must work even harder to keep it. Instead of working 50 hours a week—which is already a lot—you're putting in at least 60. Your family rarely sees you. You go into the office early and come home after they're in bed. But that's only the beginning.

Since the promotion, you've gotten a big head. Pride has swelled up in your heart and you've allowed selfishness and greed to reign. More and more things come into your life that weren't an issue before the promotion.

Because you thought about the ramifications, you realized you were in the wrong. Though a promotion is not inherently bad, you made it far more about your own gain than anything else. You used this as an opportunity to repent to God and move forward.

This is what I did when I kept praying for the pastoral position. I imagined what would've happened if he did give me the position. Lord knows I would have made a complete wreck of the church, my marriage, and my family.

Not Listening to God

Another way we sin in prayer is by stubbornly praying for something God is clearly saying no to. It's not a matter of "not yet" but flat out "no." God doesn't want us to wait, to keep asking, or to persevere in prayer. It's pretty clear the answer is no. But when we keep praying—even amid a clear "no" from God—we reveal a sense of stubbornness, a stench of sin. We want something so bad that we're going to keep asking, even when God has made himself abundantly clear.

I realize now God was telling me no several times and I simply didn't want to believe it. There were many indicators and I basically ignored them all. I had convinced myself I was ready. One Sunday, I was preaching at that church to fill in. During announcements, the deacon began by saying, "And please pray for our pastoral search; we are having a hard time finding candidates." I didn't look at my wife because I thought she might not have noticed it. But I did.

Before that day I was excited about the prospect of being a pastor there. Like I said, I had convinced myself I was ready and that this was God's plan, even though the warning signs were there. But after I preached that day, I told Shale on the way home I am not sure this is right. The church obviously wasn't interested in me like I thought they would be. They had invited me to preach three times and never made mention of the fact that I applied for the position. I simply wasn't on their radar.

That was a clear sign from God saying, "Are you going to listen to me now?" I felt embarrassed. And frustrated. But I was also upset that I was stubborn with God and myself. I wanted the position so badly I was willing to ignore clear signs from God that this wasn't the right time.

I think it's safe to say we all do this, because we're all sinners. We're stubborn, hardheaded, and think we know best. Even when God is clearly telling us no in some form, we proceed with what we want.

Putting on a Show

"And when you pray, you must not be like the hypocrites," Jesus told the disciples in Matthew 6:5. "For they love to stand and pray in the synagogues and at the street corners, that they may be seen by others." Jesus was referring to the Pharisees, who made it their life's work for others to see them praying. It made them appear extra spiritual.

Jesus continues, "And when you pray, do not heap up empty phrases as the Gentiles do, for they think that they will be heard for their many words. Do not be like them, for your Father knows what you need before you ask him." These two parts—praying for people to see and praying fancily—reveal a lot about the state of our hearts. Again, we've all done this. We want people to see us praying, as it makes us look super spiritual. It puffs up our egos, increases our pride, and makes us feel superior. But does this mean there is something wrong with praying in public? Of course not. We should pray in public—pray before your meal at a restaurant, pray with others in evangelism, pray at sporting events when the moment is right. Those things are great witnesses to a surrounding world that has neglected, ignored, and forgotten the sacred and holy.

It's when we do these things to appear a certain way that we need to be careful. Prayer becomes more of a theatrical performance rather than sincere communion with God.

To make matters worse, we not only try to look super spiritual, but sound it too. We use theological jargon and try to sound eloquent instead of praying from the heart.

All of this to make ourselves feel superior to others.

Sinning in Prayer

Whether it's praying with wrong motives, not listening to the Lord, or praying to be seen and heard, it's quite easy for us to sin in prayer—because it's quite easy for us to sin. This is why we should be all the more prudent about our motives, even while praying.

I don't intend for this chapter to be overtly negative, so don't look at this as me bashing you in the head with your sin. Instead, consider this chapter an opportunity to look in the mirror and understand both the depths of our depravity and the beauty of repentance.

Responding with Repentance

"It is a great duty," Puritan Thomas Watson once penned, "incumbent upon Christians solemnly to repent and turn unto God."[23] Sometimes repentance—turning from sin and turning to God—is the proper response to unanswered prayer. God tells us no in order to show us our sin. When he does, hopefully respond accordingly and repent. When our repentance is genuine, it is the most beautiful thing because it shows the Holy Spirit is working in us.

---

[23] Thomas Watson, *The Doctrine of Repentance* 7th Edition *(Edinburgh: Banner of Truth, 2016), 13.*

How can we tell if our repentance is sincere? Let's get some more help from Watson.

The puritan explains in his treatise on repentance that true repentance—wrought by the Holy Spirit—is a "spiritual medicine made up of six special ingredients."[24] Watson goes on:

1. Sight of sin,
2. Sorrow for sin,
3. Confession of sin,
4. Shame for sin,
5. Hatred for sin, and
6. Turning from sin.[25]

The progression of true repentance is simple. We must see our sin in order to truly repent. If we neglect to notice it, then repentance is impossible. We will never see the need for repentance if we never see the insidious nature of our sin. But even if we see our sin, we must have genuine sorrow over said sin. "Godly sorrow brings repentance that leads to salvation and leaves no regret," Paul writes in 2 Corinthians 7:10, "but worldly sorrow brings death." True, Holy Spirit-produced repentance reveals itself in authentic sorrow. If there is no *sorrow for* sin, there is no *repentance of* sin. And Paul makes his point even scarier: worldly sorrow leads to death. This worldly sorrow can reveal itself in saying, "I'm sorry, Lord, I repent," and then proceeding to do the same thing, over and over again. It's mere lip service. Put bluntly, it can reveal you're faking it. And we can't fake out God. We may say we repent as our response to unanswered prayer, but if we don't truly mean it, God sees that.

Watson adds to the list confession, shame and hatred for sin. All of these are indeed true. Repentance, for it to be sincere, must include confession—to God and (sometimes) to others—

---
[24] Ibid, 18.
[25] Ibid, 18.

shame, and hatred. We can't repent of sin if we don't admit we've been doing it. Repentance will never come if we habitually conceal our sin. And the more we conceal, the worse things get.

Furthermore, repentance is only possible when shame is present. Not shame for who we are—as we're in Christ, where there is no shame—but shame for our sin. Shame that this sin still resides in us. Shame that, even while being in Christ, we still displease our Father.

And lastly, if we are to truly repent, we must turn. We must make an about-turn. It is imperative that we do a complete 180—away from our sin and to Christ. Away from our need for approval and to Jesus, who already approves. Away from our itch to control things and to Christ, who controls all. Away from our incessant need to lie to Christ, who is the truth. Christians must do this once at conversion and then everyday while we're in Christ. We must repent daily even as children of God because sin is stealthy. To be sure, we don't continually repent to seek God's favor, but because we've already received it.

We must remember that all repentance is a gift from God (Acts 11:18; 2 Tim. 2:25). The repentance we exercise is not our own, but from the gracious hands of our Father.

Repentance and Unanswered Prayer

When God doesn't answer our prayers, we should take it as an opportunity for reflection. Are our hearts in the right place? Are we genuinely trying to pray in accordance with God's will? If we can't answer yes to those two questions, we might need to repent. That repentance will look different for each person. Maybe you need to repent of selfishness; maybe another needs to repent of greed. Or I may need to repent of ungodly ambition. Whatever the case may be, pray for God to grant you repentance and move forward. You will come to find out that one of the greatest ways God molds you more into the image of his Son is through unanswered prayer.

Prayer of Reflection

Father, forgive me. As your child, I know you've forgiven me of all my sins—you don't count them against me; I am no longer condemned (Rom. 8:1). But that doesn't mean I stop asking for forgiveness for the times I sin in my Christian walk. Repentance should be a daily habit because sin is a daily vice. Help me do so, Lord. In Jesus's name, amen.

6

Lord, I Won't Stop Praying

Responding with Persistence

JUSTIN BECAME A Christian his freshman year of college. Immediately he had a newfound love for Christ and the gospel and desired to tell everybody he knew about it—including his unbelieving, atheistic friend, Bryan. He knew that Bryan, stubborn as a mule, was not going to take too kindly to this news. Argument after argument, Justin attempted to explain why there was not only a God, but only the God of the Bible. He would then get to the gospel and witness to his friend. But alas, time after time, Justin still wouldn't believe. He wasn't convinced. So Justin decided to lay off. This didn't mean Justin was done witnessing to Bryan, but it meant he wouldn't press the issue in every interaction. Instead, he began to fervently pray for God to save his friend.

Years went by and Bryan was still an atheist. But that didn't mean Justin stopped praying. He prayed daily for God to change Bryan's stony heart into a fleshly one (Ezekiel

36:26); he even let Bryan know he was praying for it. Decades passed and both Justin and Bryan were in their 60s. All hope seemed to be lost—until one day. On one cold winter morning, Justin got a phone call. It was Bryan. He had called Justin to let him know he had become a Christian. He had recently been involved in a near-fatal car accident. During his long stay in the intensive care unit, with nowhere else to turn, Bryan had begun to pray. That praying morphed into curiosity, which led to questions. And more questions finally led to a breaking point: the conviction of sin and the need for a Savior.

Justin, now the pastor of a small Southern Baptist church in their town, was absolutely floored—and understandably so! Through many tears and smiles, all Justin could say to Bryan was, "God answers prayer."

God Honors Persistence

In the above story, Justin was determined to consistently pray for Bryan. There were many points when Justin thought all hope was lost. If God hadn't saved Bryan yet, he wasn't going to now. He knew that was a sinful way to think, however, so he continued to pray; he knew God could save anybody he pleases. After decades upon decades of God telling him no, God finally answered his prayer. He "finally" saved Bryan![26] But what was so admirable about Justin was he kept praying. Through years of what seemed to be God ignoring him or not answering his prayer, he continued to pray, continued to plead, continued to ask. It wasn't through stubbornness or unwillingness to move on, but through belief that God can save anybody—even somebody like Bryan. And he knew, through the testimony of Scripture, God uses prayer as a means for salvation. So he kept faithfully praying. And then it happened.

---

[26] To be sure, I put *finally* in quotation marks because, to God, Bryan's salvation wasn't past due. God saved Bryan's exactly when he planned to save him.

God honors persistent prayer. He is pleased when his children come to him again and again to ask for things—even the same thing, like Justin.

Faithfulness vs. Stubbornness

There is an important distinction to make in this chapter that needs to be understood. In calling the reader—and myself—to respond to unanswered prayer with persistence, I am not meaning to be stubborn. In an earlier chapter, I kept praying for a pastoral vacancy but, in stubbornness, I kept praying though God was clearly telling me no. I wanted *my* plan to work out so badly that I was willing to be stubborn and ignore clear direction from the Lord.

This is not what I am referring to here.

In this chapter I want to talk about us responding to unanswered prayer with persistence or perseverance. Not like me—with a hard head and distrust in God's providence; but like Justin—with trust in God's providence and promises. He doesn't see a stubborn heart, but a prayerful heart—a heart that is deeply in awe of God. A heart that knows God uses prayer to accomplish his will. And when that awe invades the heart, we are willing to pray for the same thing over and over and over again. We believe with all our heart that God is faithful to his promises. Praying for the same thing habitually doesn't guarantee God will eventually answer it, but it does mean God sees our faithfulness in prayer. It shows we truly believe him to be sovereign, to be in control, to be God.

The Persistent Widow

Scripture is full of passages showing persistence in prayer. For example, the story of the persistence widow in Luke's Gospel:

> And he told them a parable to the effect that they ought always to pray and not lose heart. He said, "In

a certain city there was a judge who neither feared God nor respected man. And there was a widow in that city who kept coming to him and saying, 'Give me justice against my adversary.' For a while he refused, but afterward he said to himself, 'Though I neither fear God nor respect man, yet because this widow keeps bothering me, I will give her justice, so that she will not beat me down by her continual coming.'" And the Lord said, "Hear what the unrighteous judge says. And will not God give justice to his elect, who cry to him day and night? Will he delay long over them? I tell you, he will give justice to them speedily. Nevertheless, when the Son of Man comes, will he find faith on earth? (Luke 18:18)

The judge didn't grant the widow's wishes because he truly believed in her request but simply because he was tired of her asking. And yet, God never gets tired with us. He never gets bothered.

We can be this persistent with God and be comforted he will never get annoyed. No changing the subject, no rolling of eyes, no exasperating. God wants us to come to him—over and over and over again. Those moments of unanswered prayer—in the proper circumstance—should prompt you to keep praying for it until you can't pray anymore. Don't lose hope, never give up. There's no such thing as going to God too many times. God still works even through unanswered prayer. When God tells us no, it's less about why he did and more about how we respond. Will we want to know the reason he said no? Absolutely. And don't be afraid to ask that.

The late J.I. Packer has a great word on this:

Perhaps he means to strengthen us in patience, good humor, compassion, humility or meekness . . . Perhaps he has new lessons in self-denial and self-distrust to teach us. Perhaps he wishes to break us of complacency or undetected forms of pride and conceit. Perhaps His purpose is simply to draw us closer to himself . . . Or perhaps God is preparing us for forms of service of which at present we have no inkling.[27]

If we truly trust the Lord, however, then we don't *need* to know why. We trust him—and that's enough. What we do know is God wants us to feel free to come to him—anytime, any place, anywhere. And it doesn't matter if it's the 500th time you've prayed for it. He wants your heart. He desires your affection, your trust, your confidence in him. So though your parents may have gotten annoyed with you or you get annoyed with your children, Scripture is clear that we cannot annoy our Heavenly Father. Therefore, go to him. Repeatedly. Non-stop. Without end. Ask, request, plead—he wants to hear from you!

There is another component to this we need to understand. Satan plays a role. He is crafty (Gen. 3:1) and wants you to believe you are annoying God. He wants to put it in your mind that you are driving God crazy, that all God wants to do is cover his ears when you pray. Nothing could be further from the truth. Do you remember chapter 1? It's not as if God has had enough and he's just dealing with your constant groaning, your annoying neediness. No, he's listening. He's not covering his ears, but leaning in closer. Don't believe Satan's lies. Keep going to the Lord.

A Persevering Hope

Christians hope. This hope isn't like the rest of the world's hope—one of wishful thinking, of hoping for the best. The Christian hope is based on Christ, on the promises of redemption. It's not a mere crossing of the fingers, but a certain-

---

[27] J.I. Packer, *Knowing God* 20th Anniversary edition (Downers Grove: IVP Books, 193), 97.

ty. And our Heavenly Father never wants us to second-guess this hope—even when our prayers go unanswered.

When we are praying for something—and praying hard for it—it can be easy to lose hope when God tells us no. We become frustrated, worn-out, and exhausted. But in those moments of frustration and exhaustion is when God wants us to persevere in prayer with hope-filled hearts. He wants us to keep asking, no matter the outcome. Our faithful prayers reveal if we truly trust him.

Let's think about this from a real-world perspective. Imagine your spouse just got diagnosed with stage-four brain cancer. From a purely scientific standpoint, the odds are slim—there's practically no hope. Yet, as a person of sincere and abiding faith in God, you pray. You pray everyday for your spouse to be healed. And everyday, she gets worse. Everyday her condition deteriorates. You believe God can heal her but, as of that moment, he hasn't. Then you start to get discouraged and upset. Who wouldn't be? You see that God is not answering your prayer and you become disheartened.

What should you do in this situation? Stop praying? By every indication, your spouse is about to pass away and God isn't answering your prayer. Or do you become persistent in prayer and keep asking, keep pleading, keep crying out to the Lord through your stream of tears? You know he doesn't guarantee good health, but you know he is a God of miracles and can heal anybody of anything. So you keep praying despite knowing all your prayers for present-day, this-world healing could go unanswered. Nevertheless, you are certain, beyond a shadow of a doubt, that she will experience ultimate healing the moment she passes into the presence of Jesus in glory.

You know God will either perform miraculous healing or will rid her of sin when she passes.

Either way, God is good.

The Persistence of Abraham Regarding Sodom and Gomorrah

Let's turn our attention to another biblical story of persistent prayer. God is about to destroy Sodom and Gomorrah for its rampant wickedness, but Abraham intercedes for them.

So the men turned from there and went toward Sodom, but Abraham still stood before the Lord. Then Abraham drew near and said, "Will you indeed sweep away the righteous with the wicked? Suppose there are fifty righteous within the city. Will you then sweep away the place and not spare it for the fifty righteous who are in it? Far be it from you to do such a thing, to put the righteous to death with the wicked, so that the righteous fare as the wicked! Far be that from you! Shall not the Judge of all the earth do what is just?" And the Lord said, "If I find at Sodom fifty righteous in the city, I will spare the whole place for their sake." Abraham answered and said, "Behold, I have undertaken to speak to the Lord, I who am but dust and ashes. Suppose five of the fifty righteous are lacking. Will you destroy the whole city for lack of five?" And he said, "I will not destroy it if I find forty-five there." Again he spoke to him and said, "Suppose forty are found there." He answered, "For the sake of forty I will not do it." Then he said, "Oh let not the Lord be angry, and I will speak. Suppose thirty are found there." He answered, "I will not do it, if I find thirty there." He said, "Behold, I have undertaken to speak to the Lord. Suppose twenty are found there." He answered, "For the sake of twenty I will not destroy it." Then he said, "Oh let not the Lord be angry, and I will speak again but this once. Suppose ten are found there." He answered, "For the sake of ten I will not destroy it." And the Lord went his way, when he had finished speaking to Abraham, and Abraham returned to his place. (Genesis 18:22-33

This passage of Scripture is infamous because of the homosexual debauchery of Sodom and Gomorrah. But have we ever noticed the amount of times Abraham pleads for God to not destroy them?

Abraham pleads with God six times regarding the destruction of Sodom and Gomorrah. Of course, it turned out that there was not one righteous person there, but God still made the promise. This is a wonderful example of the perseverance God loves to see from his children. Abraham wasn't being hardheaded or stubborn, but merely believed God's character. He knew God loves to hear the persistent pleading of his children. That doesn't mean he will wind up answering our prayers, but it means he takes great delight in our prayers of faith. At the end of the day, the goal is to become more like Christ in the process.

Think of that one thing in your life you've prayed for multiple times and it hasn't come to fruition yet. Perhaps it's finding the right spouse. Maybe it's getting a clean bill of health that you haven't had in years. Whatever the case may be, God doesn't want us to stop praying. He wants our knees to be scuffed from praying so much. What he doesn't want us to do is become idle. He wants us, in the midst of unanswered prayer, to continue praying, to keep pleading, to never stop asking. The persistence of our prayers reveals the faithfulness of our hearts.

God doesn't want us to become idle in our prayer life simply because he didn't answer our prayers. When times get tough, God wants us to pray more and ask more—not less. He wants us to trust him. He wants us to seek him more, not less. Unanswered prayer—whatever it's for—is always discouraging. But sometimes, even when he says no, he invites us to continue asking, continue pleading, continue seeking. God loves to listen to the persistent, faithful, believing cries of his children.

Prayer of Reflection

Father, you tell me not to stop praying—so I won't. I will continue to believe you will heal, you will deliver, and you will save. I know from your Word you honor godly persistence. So, by your Spirit, help me to keep going, keep pushing, keep pleading. Even when it's tough. In Jesus's name, amen.

7

Lord, I Will Draw Near

Responding with Coming Closer to God

UNANSWERED PRAYER can be excruciating. If we're not careful, it can seem like God has completely abandoned us, left us without any hope. But we know from God's Word that's not true. We know God's character. What we know about God supplants what we may sometimes feel about God. We know he's good (Psalm 25:8), righteous (Psalm 119:137), and faithful to his promises (Psalm 145:13), even when our feelings say he's ignoring us.

Our natural instinct is to withdraw, turn away, and shrink back when God tells us no. Our first step is backward, not forward. Instead of digging in, we give up. Rather than pushing forward, we retreat back. We despair, pout, and, depending on the situation, get angry. But we should know by now that God never turns away from the cries, pleas, and supplications of his children. In fact, it's quite the opposite. He is eager to hear our prayers. The sound of our prayers is a beautiful noise. And it gets even better: he loves listening to our prayers even when he says no them. It's not as if he throws the unanswered prayers in a divine trash can. No, God wants us to respond to unanswered prayer by pushing further into him, by drawing nearer.

This is a sign of genuine faith. No matter the difficulty—even via unanswered prayer—we push on forward. We lean into him. We keep marching toward him by faith because we know what Scripture says and we know how fickle our emotions can be. We rely on the unbreakable foundation of the Bible rather than the uneasy waves of our feelings.

So, you might ask, *if God wants us to come closer to him even after he tells us no, how do we do that?* In what can seem to be the most difficult time of our lives—where our whole life is falling apart—how in the world do we draw closer to God?

Four words. *The means of grace*. What are the means of grace? They're how we commune with our God and grow as Christians.

Reading Scripture

Do you want to hear from God? Read the Bible. Don't just read it like a newspaper or the daily sports column. Don Whitney, in his timeless work *Spiritual Disciplines for the Christian Life*, writes that

> Far too many read the Bible publicly in such a flat, unenthusiastic way that it sounds like a book no one would want to read on his or her own. Read it for what it is: the living Word of the Living God.[28]

The Bible isn't meant to be read like any 'ole book. It's read so we may be transformed. You will not grow as a Christian if you do not read your Bible. And what a privilege it is that we have personal copies of Scripture! It's shameful we don't read it as much. It collects dust more than it collects our tears of

---

[28] Donald S. Whitney, *Spiritual Disciplines for the Christian Life (Colorado Springs: NavPress, 2014), 25.

repentance or joy. God wants us to know him more and the primary way we do that is by reading his Word.

However, many Christians find the Bible difficult to read. We become distracted because our attention span is short or we have our iPhone nearby begging to be picked up.

Simply put, reading the Bible isn't as big of a priority as it should be. When that's the case, unanswered prayer will perhaps be more prevalent in our lives because we're not as close to God as we should be. We're his children, yes, but we don't give him the attention, affection, admiration, and trust he deserves. Our sin is fracturing our relationship with him, and so our prayers become so superficial. We must remember that our prayers reveal where our hearts reside. It can display our idols. God is less concerned with answering our weak prayers as he is with us coming nearer to him in faith.

We know we grow closer to him by reading our Bibles. But the book is so large and intimidating, where do we even begin? And when we do start, we don't really understand what we're reading, so we just stick with the verses we learned in Sunday school years ago. However, the presence of intimidation and confusion doesn't mean we just give up; it doesn't mean we stop trying. We become more like Jesus through drudgery, not ease. Through trials, not triumphs. Through pain, not health. God wants us to dive into the pages of Scripture as we respond to unanswered prayer so we may come to know him more.

So how can we do that?

Read the gospels. If we read any part of the Bible with the goal of knowing God more intimately, it will happen. He promises us that. But if we want to encounter Christ anew, we must soak our minds with the gospels: Matthew, Mark, Luke, and John. As I write these words I am currently reading Matthew in my daily reading. I felt somewhat stagnant in my walk with the Lord and wanted to encounter him once more and be renewed by Christ's work. So I committed to reading the four gospel accounts—because that's where we explicitly find Jesus. If you want to know God more deeply and cherish him more affectionately, I suggest beginning with the gospels.[29]

Fasting

I am abysmal at fasting—in more than one way. First, I very rarely fast. It's easy to go along with the consumer-driven culture. We are natural consumers—of food, of entertainment, of *everything*. And Christians (like myself) are the same way, though we are called to be different.

With that being said, what does it mean to fast, anyway? To lean on the words of Donald Whitney again, he says that

> Christian fasting is a believer's *voluntary* abstinence from food for spiritual purposes.... It is voluntary in that fasting should not be coerced. And fasting is more than just the ultimate crash diet for the body; it is *abstinence from food* for *spiritual* purposes (italics original).[30]

To do a Christian fast you must have a spiritual purpose in mind. And yes, strictly speaking, a Christian fast is from food. However, there is nothing wrong with fasting from other things as well. Martyn Lloyd-Jones echoes this sentiment by saying

> To make the matter complete, we would add that fasting, if we conceive of it truly, must not only be confined to the question of food and drink; fasting

---

[29] One of the best things you can do is pick one book of the Bible—1 John, for example—and read it for a month. Since 1 John is a relatively small book, you can likely read the whole book in one sitting. Commit yourself to reading it in whole—or at least every other day—for a whole month. You will come to know that book inside and out. Even better, you will come to know God more deeply. Of course, it doesn't have to be 1 John. Pick any book. Just commit to being in that book for a month to really saturate yourself in it. You have your whole life to read the whole Bible. Take your time.

[30] Ibid, 192.

should really be made to include abstinence from anything which is legitimate in and of itself for the sake of some special spiritual purpose. There are many bodily functions which are right and normal and perfectly legitimate, but which for special peculiar reasons in certain circumstances should be controlled. That is fasting.[31]

I have fasted from food as a Christian before, but usually when I fast, I do so from social media. Why? Because social media grips my attention more so than food. Even though I have an unhealthy diet—too much fast food anybody?—I am far more attached to social media. And on occasion, it's time to abstain to reorient my mind.

Fasting is intricately connected with prayer. Here's what happens if we're fasting from social media. We are bored and feel the tug to pick up our phones, open Twitter, and mindlessly scroll until we're bored again. Then we turn to Instagram then Facebook—rinse and repeat. When we fast, the goal is to pray as soon as we feel that urge. Our knees should be bloody when we fast from praying so much. As we desire to get on social media, we go to the Lord in prayer, asking for guidance, strength, and forgiveness. We want guidance to help navigate fasting and our lives as Christians in general. We want strength because, if we admit it, we are very weak creatures and need the Lord's strength to push us through. Lastly, we ask for forgiveness, because we know we've sinned far too many times, in too many ways.

When God says no to our prayers, take it as an opportunity to fast.

Local Church Fellowship

Nowadays the necessity of the local church has been thrown out the theological window. When online church is running

---

[31] D. Martyn Lloyd-Jones, *Studies in the Sermon on the Mount* (Grand Rapids: Eerdmans, 1960), vol. 1, 38.

rampant, it's all the more important to understand why being in church—in-person with other like-minded believers—is drastically important.

I think all Christians understand the value of living in community with other followers of Christ. To advance in our Christian walk we must be a part of a local church where we are surrounded by people who care for us and want to see us thrive.[32]

When our prayers go unanswered, it ought to be a wake-up call to dive back into the means of grace God has mercifully provided for us. One of those means of grace is the local church. Fellowship with like-minded Christians in the gathering of the local church is crucial to a Christian's spiritual life.

Are you in a desperate moment in your walk with God? Do you feel like you're living in a spiritual wasteland? All the more reason to be plugged into a local church. Your need for community is just that—a need. Listen, I don't need a Redbull, but I want one. I don't need to eat a whole bag of Doritos, but I sure want to. Fellowship in the local church is not merely a want, but a need. And it certainly needs to be a *want* first.

Our sanctification will be put to a jarring halt if we neglect fellowship in the local church. And I am not even talking about sitting under preaching or taking part in communion (though those are extremely important). I am referring to the community aspect of the local church. Sanctification—growing more holy everyday—is a community project. We can't win that "game" on our own. We need the Spirit's help; but the Spirit has put us in a church surrounded by believers to help us grow.

It's kind of like this. If you have asthma, then there will be times when you're in desperate need of your inhaler. If

---

[32] This idea is explored more extensive in Joe Thorn's book, *The Life of the Church: The Table, Pulpit, and Square* (Chicago: Moody Publishers, 2017), 19.

you are struggling to breath but refuse to use your inhaler, that will lead to dire circumstances for your health. The same is true with our need for fellowship in the local church. We won't survive as Christians without the local church.

You won't be alone if you take that burden with unanswered prayer to the local church. Unanswered prayer is an experience every Christian deals with. Perhaps at your church's next prayer meeting—if you have one—bring up your burden and how, at the moment, it seems as though God is telling you no. I promise you will be met with mutual encouragement from other Christians. On the other hand, they may be able to talk you through why, perhaps, God didn't answer your prayer.

This is why it's so important to experience this fellowship. Yes, there are people who annoy you, pester you, and simply get under your skin. Honestly, you may be the annoying one. *I* might be the annoying one. But that's part of the process. It's one big family—family that's far deeper than blood. But just because there are people who talk different, act different, and think different than you doesn't mean God can't or won't use them to speak truth into your life.

Get Closer to the Lord

When God tells us no, he's not scolding us or angry with us. He is beckoning us to come to him. He is drawing us closer to himself, pleading with us to trust him even amidst unanswered prayer. We will not grow closer to the Lord by conjuring up some image in our head or having some mystical experience. We get closer to the Lord as his children by saturating ourselves with the means of grace.

Don't take God saying no as a bad thing. Take it as a call to lay down your desires at the moment and run to him. Flee from the sin that may be entangling you (Hebrews 12:1) and collapse in the arms of Jesus. Get to know him more. He is waiting.

Prayer of Reflection

Father, draw me closer to you. I know I am your child, but I neglect your means of grace far too often. My heart grows cold quickly and it scares me. Give me the strength, the grace, the motivation to read your Word, to pray more, and to enjoy fellowship with other believers. I know I need it, but many times my heart doesn't want it. Please help me with that. In Jesus's name, amen.

8

Lord, Thank You

Responding with Thankfulness

IF I HAD STAYED at my first church, I would be a pastor right now. In fact, I would've been a pastor at the ripe age of 21. I was in my denomination's school of ministry program; once finished, I would get immediately get assigned to a local church. Or, I would at least immediately begin looking for one. Finishing the coursework means you got the stamp of approval from the denomination—you're ready for ministry! Of course, being qualified for the pastorate is not that simple, but I was naïve then.

I prayed and prayed for God to help me finish my work and plug me into a good church. I had my life planned out. Everything was running smoothly. But then—as I said in the previous chapter—God had other plans. The more I studied, the more I understood I was in the wrong denomination. I loved the people in our church but my theological views were different—too different. Right before we left the church, I remember having a discussion with my then-pastor about my predicament. I was a full-blown, five-point Calvinist[33] attempting to train for ministry in a Pentecostal church. I remember asking my pastor, "Do you know what Calvinism is?" He let out a sigh while halfway rolling his eyes, "Yes, I do."

"Well," I said, "I am one."

My belief in the doctrines of grace was likely going to be an issue, but it wasn't my biggest issue. I had problems with their stance on the sign gifts, and I had a huge problem with their view on women in ministry. At the time I actually wanted to stay in the program. After awhile, though, I realized it simply wasn't going to work. My theology simply wasn't charismatic. Not only did I need to get out of their school of ministry, I needed to leave the church.

I say all that to say this. Thank God he didn't answer my prayer of getting into the pastorate. It would have been a complete disaster. Even though the desire was there, I was not ready. Even though I was discouraged by his "no" at the time, I am so thankful for it today.

As much as unanswered prayer hurts, we should be thankful for it. There are many times that, if our prayer were answered, we'd almost immediately regret it. Why is that? Put simply, we know less than God. God, the one who answers (or doesn't answer) our prayers, is also the one who knows all things. He is infinitely wise, and we are infinitely clueless about life.

There are many reasons to be thankful for unanswered prayer, but let's briefly go over four.

Thankful for Life

Every breath we take is a gift from God. From our first cry as an infant to our final breath, all of life is given from the gracious hands of our Father.

---

[33] Cage-stage, if I'm honest. If you'd like a primer on what it means to be a cage-stage Calvinist, read this article: https://www.challies.com/sponsored/7-signs-that-youre-a-cage-stage-calvinist/.

When playing golf, my dad was my biggest coach and fan. (Sometimes I didn't want his coaching!) I knew he wanted me to succeed. But sometimes I would throw temper tantrums on the golf course and would have a sorry attitude the rest of the day. When the timing was right, he would always reiterate to me what he learned from a friend of his: ES, EM, ED—which means Every Second, Every Minute, Every Day. He continuously reminded me to live my life to the fullest every second I have. And under the sovereign care of my Heavenly Father, I knew it was my duty, my obligation to be thankful for every last second—because every last second is a gift from the Lord.

But even this attitude is countercultural. We live in a day and age of ungratefulness, of irritableness, of plain 'ole grumpiness. Christians are called by God to stand out like a sore thumb. And these days all we have to do is be perpetually thankful.

When God says no to our prayers, we shouldn't get frustrated but should be thankful—thankful he has given us life and continues to sustain us.

Thankful for God's Sovereign Will

God is sovereign, and I am not. That fact right there should cause an immense amount of gratitude to swell up in my heart. God's will for our lives—his perfect will—is unchangeable. Man lives his life, but God plans it all. See for yourself.

> Many are the plans in the mind of a man, but it is the purpose of the Lord that will stand (Proverbs 19:21).
>
> The heart of man plans his way, but the Lord establishes his steps (Proverbs 16:9).
>
> The plans of the heart belong to man, but the answer of the tongue is from the Lord (Proverbs 16:1).
>
> Commit your work to the Lord, and your plans will be established. The Lord has made everything for

its purpose, even the wicked for the day of trouble (Proverbs 16:3-4).

Your eyes saw my unformed substance; in you book were written every one of them, the days that were formed for me, when as yet there was none of them (Psalm 139:16).

Many people—even well meaning Christians—balk at the idea of God controlling every last minute detail of life. They say he is sovereign . . . but how sovereign? "If there is one single atom in this universe running around loose, totally free of God's sovereignty," the late R.C. Sproul once wrote, "then we have no guarantee that a single promise of God will ever be fulfilled."[34]

Scripture is pretty clear. For God to be sovereign he must be sovereign over all. Though this book isn't about the sovereignty of God, we should be thankful for his sovereignty as it's expressed in his perfect will. There is not one thing, not one animal, not one human invention, not one person that freely roams outside the sovereign control of God. And that is a good thing, because we serve a good God. And our good God does whatever he wants (Ps. 115:3).

Commenting on Psalm 115:3, John Piper wrote in his famous work *Desiring God: Meditations of a Christian Hedonist*,

> The implication of this text is that God has the right and power to do whatever makes Him happy. That is what it means to say that God is sovereign. Think about it for a moment: If God is sovereign and can do anything He pleases, then none of His purposes can be frustrated.[35]

---

[34] R.C. Sproul, *Chosen by God: Knowing God's Perfect Plan of His Glory and His Children* (Carol Stream: Tyndale House Publishers, 1986) 16.
[35] John Piper, *Desiring God: Meditations of a Christian Hedonist* (Colorado Springs: Multnomah, 1983), 32.

We must understand that the whole Christian life is linked to the sovereignty of God. From regeneration—where the Holy Spirit gives us a new heart (Ezekiel 36:26)—to glorification—when God rids us of sin in Heaven—God is the one behind it all, working everything according to the counsel of his will (Eph. 1). And this even comes down all the way to the practicalities of dealing with unanswered prayer.

Think of it like this. Since God is sovereign, not only should we trust that he has the best in mind for us, but we can also be thankful when he doesn't answer our prayer. Why? Because we know, if he did, something would happen that wouldn't be in his will for us.

If God says no outright, he does so sovereignly. If God says, "just wait," he does so sovereignly. If God says, "that's not the right thing to ask for," he does so sovereignly.

But Blake, you might ask, *what if he says no to my prayer asking for my suffering to abate?*

This may intertwine with the previous chapter, but this question ultimately depends on what we believe about God. This is why the sovereignty of God is the most practical doctrine we believe. Do we believe God controls everything—down to the tiniest atom? If so, we must believe he is sovereign over our suffering, or our spouse's suffering, or our friend's suffering. When the going gets tough, God is still sovereign. And, yes, sometimes God sovereignly says no to our pleas for suffering to end. What he wants from us in those moments is to trust him even when our world is crashing down. If that suffering leads to death, we know—more than anything else in this world—that "to live is Christ, and to die is gain" (Phil. 1:21).

When God says no to our prayers, take a moment to reflect on his sovereign reign and rule over all things. If he is sovereignly saying no to our prayers, there's a reason. And we should trust him.

Thankful He Knows my Needs

Part of God caring for his children (1 Peter 5:7) is the glorious truth that he will provide all we need. As he tells us in Matthew's Gospel, he knows what we need. If he faithfully cares for the birds of the sky and the flowers in the ground, don't we think he will take care of us all the more? We have far more value than birds and flowers. God's got us.

With that said, we must address an issue here that falls entirely on our backs. Too many times we fall prey to thinking our *wants* and *desires* are truly needs. God does not promise to provide all we want; he promises to give us all we need. This issue correlates directly with unanswered prayer. We may pray for something we perceive as a need only to find our prayer go unanswered. Then we become discouraged, frustrated, and confused. *I thought God would supply my every need?* we might ask. Indeed, this is true. God supplies all our needs (Philippians 4:19). But we mistakenly believe what we're praying for is a need, not merely a desire. And instead of being thankful to God for his grace, love, mercy, and fatherly care, we become resentful and angry. This is why it's imperative to learn how to differentiate between a *want* and a *need*.

Truth be told, we don't need many things in this life. We Western Christians have it made. We are filthy rich compared to the rest of the world. And yet, we are perpetually dissatisfied because there is always a new fad, a new toy, a new something. Our consumer-driven society has drawn us into the sinful fray of believing everything is a need, not a want. We must renew our minds, as Paul exhorts us to do in Romans 12:2. We must not be conformed to this world; we must be different. And that comes all the way down to how our heart posture is. Are we consistently thankful or habitually ungrateful?

When God tells us no, let us not respond with resentment, but thankfulness. If we believe the Bible—which we should—then we know God supplies all our needs. We will never go without what we truly need. As our Heavenly Father, God takes extraordinary care of us. Unanswered prayer shouldn't be met with annoyance or hurt, but thankfulness.

Thankful He Sent His Son

The most beautiful act of love ever shown is God the Father sending God the Son into the world to die in the place of those who would believe (John 3:16). It's unfathomable, breathtaking, out-of-this-world. What incredible love God has for us, filthy sinners. The love of God displayed in the life, death, and resurrection of Jesus is simply glorious.

John MacArthur said it perfectly:

> The second member of the Trinity would take on all the weakness and infirmity (yet not sin) of human nature and would secure for his people the righteousness, forgiveness, and cleansing that they could never obtain for themselves.[36]

Evangelicals focus heavily on Jesus's death on the cross and subsequent resurrection—which we absolutely should!—but sometimes we do so at the expense of a vitally important truth: Jesus was without sin (Hebrews 4:15). His sinless life was just as important as his atoning death.

MacArthur again:

> He would live as a man in perfect obedience to the Father, die on the cross as a substitutionary sacrifice to atone for the sins of those whom the Father had chosen, and rise again in victory over sin and death, all in the power of the Holy Spirit. Redemption would be accomplished by the miraculous incarna-

---

[36] John Macarthur and Richard Mayhue ed., *Biblical Doctrine: A Systematic Summary of Bible Truth* (Wheaton: Crossway, 2017), 513.

tion, vicarious life, penal-substitutionary death, and death-defeating resurrection of the God-man, the Lord Jesus Christ.[37]

When we habitually remind ourselves of these precious truths, it's all the more difficult to be upset by unanswered prayer and so much easier to be thankful. Thankful for the Father sending the Son to not only die in our place, but to live for us. Thankful that we, as God's children, are the recipients of what John Newton coined as, "Amazing grace."

Unanswered prayer is going to happen, and it's going to happen more often than we'd like. Why? Because more often than not, we either pray for the wrong things, need to be patient, or something in between. And when we are faced with God telling us no, we should remind ourselves of redemption, of the cross, of the empty tomb, and be thankful.

---

[37] Ibid, 513.

Prayer of Reflection

Father, thank you for my life. Thank you for the ability to smell good aromas, taste wonderful foods, see beautiful things, hear glorious music, and so much more. Above all, Lord, thank you for sending Jesus to die for me. As I follow you—even amid unanswered prayer—I pray you help me respond with thankfulness, because I should always be thankful. In Jesus's name, amen,

9

Lord, I Will Wait for You

Responding with Patience

I GREW UP ON the golf course. I was a country club kid. If you needed to find me, I was playing golf. My first big dream was to become a professional golfer. As I grew older and realized what my talent was in high school, I knew that dream had sailed before I realized it.

So then I decided that I wanted to become a golf professional.[38] I would get a degree in college specifically in that area, get more training, and find a job somewhere and do that for the rest of my life. And as I started college, things we're looking that way.

And then God saved me.

Shortly after my conversion in 2013 as a freshman in college, I had a strong desire to enter pastoral ministry. For a moment I thought to myself, "I could become a golf professional

---

[38] Yes, there's a difference. When I say "professional golfer," think Tiger Woods. When I say, "golf professional," think the manager of a golf course.

and a pastor." Except as time went on, my desire for anything golf related vanished quicker than my chances of competing as a professional. I quit the college golf team and all my attention went to studying theology and strengthening my relationship with the Lord. Instead of learning about the golf swing, I was learning about the foundations of Christianity. And not only was I learning the fundamentals of our faith, but I was also figuring out what it means to be in ministry. So then I turned my focus solely to pastoral ministry.

And then I read James 3:1, which says, "Not many of you should become teachers, my brothers, for you know that we who teach will be judged with greater strictness." This verse squelched my supposed desire for ministry—momentarily. That desire quickly returned and I couldn't shake it off. As one who never enjoyed public speaking, I was feeling the "call" to preach and I had to express that to someone.

Once I spoke to my then-girlfriend (now my wife) about this feeling, I wanted to tell our pastor about it. He was absolutely thrilled to see such a desire for ministry in a person my age. When most teenagers are just "having fun" in college, I was going a completely different direction. Instead of parties, I was plumbing the depths of the gospel.

But then I didn't hear anything from him about it for a while. And it left me pondering if I was in over my head.

But as we strolled into church one Wednesday night, he came up to me and said, "Blake, are you ready?"

Confused, I said, "Ready for what?"

"I want you to preach next Wednesday."

Any shred of doubt was gone; all second-guessing was erased. "I will absolutely do that," I said cheerfully.

I preached my first sermon that next week. It was entitled, "What is Faith?" and came in at a quick 20 minutes. I stuck to my notes heavily, didn't look up that much, and stammered out the gate. But I enjoyed every second of it. It felt natural—where God wanted me to be.

As my desire for ministry progressed, I got the green light to enroll into my denomination's school of ministry. I would take classes for two years and, once finished, would most likely be thrown into the first church available.

Of course, that didn't happen. Theological differences arose and we decided to leave the church (as I talked about in a previous chapter). I thank God every time I think of that because, if I am honest with myself, I would've been a disaster pastoring a church at the ripe age of 22.

Seminary

As we moved to a new church, I was prepared to continue studying on my own because I knew I wouldn't be able to afford a formal seminary education. But one day my aunt came to town and told me she'd be willing to pay my tuition if I went to seminary. Who wouldn't take that offer?

After much thought and prayer, I decided to attend Midwestern Baptist Theological Seminary. Though it was online, it was still a great experience. I received my Master of Theological Studies degree in Preaching and Pastoral Ministry in 2019. And because I was so excited and eager to get into ministry, I jumped into the application process. After speaking with one of my pastors about it, I decided to submit several applications to churches around my area and even across state borders. I was hopeful. I was even interviewed for one of the positions.

But the more I thought about ministry—and the more I talked with my pastors together about it—I realized it wasn't the right time. I simply wasn't ready. I naively thought that graduating from seminary meant I was ready for ministry. That simply wasn't the case.

Be Patient

Impatience comes natural to me. I don't have to try to be impatient; it is my go-to attitude. Whether I am waiting in the drive-thru or waiting for God to answer my prayer, I am always tapping my foot with impatience.

Of course, we are clearly told in Galatians 5 that one mark of the fruit of the Spirit is patience. So when I am being impatient, I am not displaying the fruit of the Spirit; I am not being godly.

When we are impatient, it is a signal that we aren't truly trusting in God's plan and timing. Patience and trust are connected. It reveals we're yielding to our flesh, not the Spirit. We are succumbing to the temptation to direct our own lives, do things when we want, and only ask God for things when we're desperate. But that's not how God has called us to live. He has called us to live according to his good and perfect will.

At the very core, our impatience shows that we want control over our lives. And when our lives spiral out of control, we get snippy. But we weren't created to control our lives. Truth be told, no matter how much it feels like we are in control, we are not. We don't control anything. God does. He could take it all in a second—our health, our finances, our family, etc., because it all belongs to him. Ask yourself: would you trust him if he did?

Our incessant need to control everything reveals itself in the sin of impatience. And that impatience, usually, communicates many things to God.

1. Our impatience shows that we don't trust God's plan. My plan for my entire life has been different than God's plan for my life, even when I became a Christian. I had everything planned. I was going to be involved in the golf industry in some fashion and make a great career out of it. It would be a career I enjoyed and knew would support my family one day.

Easy as pie. But God had different plans, and they frustrated me. He all but eradicated my desire for golf for the longest time. I didn't really want anything to do with it. Instead of realizing he was shaping my heart and cutting an idol out of my life, I became annoyed that things weren't going my way. I simply didn't trust God's plan.

2. Our impatience shows that we don't trust God's timing. I've wanted to be in pastoral ministry for at least six years now, but it hasn't happened yet. Sometimes I get frustrated that things haven't progressed yet. However, each time God has closed a door of ministry, I wind up realizing it was for the best. I am discouraged at first when things don't work out, but in the end I understand that it simply isn't time yet. I still believe he has, in fact, called me to pastoral ministry, but I am just not ready. Sometimes it's hard to trust his timing because things look like they'd be great. But that's why we are not God. God is infinite; we are finite. God is omniscient; we know very little. *Don't we think God's timing is better than ours?*

3. Our impatience shows that we don't trust God—period. In the end, when we are impatient about anything, it reveals—at least in that very moment of impatience—that we simply don't trust God to control our lives. We don't trust his plan, his timing, or his judgment. We think we know better, hence why we're impatient. We think we ought to control our own lives, but don't we see that things would be catastrophic if that were to happen? It is only when we repent of our impatience that we show ourselves to truly be trusting God.

When our prayers go unanswered, it might not be an outright "no," but merely a "not yet." Don't lose heart; don't be discouraged. Even in our frustration and impatience, God is still working. He is still orchestrating things for our lives. Trust his answer.

Thus far, I have taken you back to the introduction a couple times to talk more about our personal experience with unanswered prayer. That day God told us no—but it wasn't an outright no. It was a "not yet," because God wound up giving us children. For one reason or another, God did not plan for us to have a child at that specific time. It was his will for us to go through a moment of grief and patience while we trust in him and his sovereign plan for our lives.

When we pray for something and God says no, we must be patient. We must trust he knows better. We must remember—and believe—that since God is omnipotent, omniscient, and omnipresent, he knows infinitely more than us. Understanding these attributes should help us be patient with the Lord.

A Lesson on God's Attributes

Let's talk about three of God's attributes briefly.

God is omnipotent. This simply means he is all-powerful. He possesses all power. There is nothing above God in strength because he has all strength. Nobody matches up with him. Nothing touches him. And he has the right to do whatever he pleases (Psalm 115:3).

He has the power to create life and end life; he has the power to bring calamity and the power to bring prosperity. He has the power to destroy his enemies and the power to bring salvation to his enemies. "I know that you can do all things," Job 42:2 reads, "and that no purpose of yours can be thwarted."

God is omniscient. This simply means he is all-knowing. He knows all things (1 John. 3:20), including our thoughts (Psalm 139:4). Better yet, all knowledge comes from him—he is the source of it all. But it's not as if he knows all things the way humans do. "God has never looked into the future and learned anything," Dr. Steven Lawson once said. If God learned something in the future, he wouldn't possess all knowledge. God knows all things, ultimately, because he ordained all things.

God is omnipresent. This simply means he is everywhere at once (Psalm 33:13-14). And not just every*where* at once, but every*when*. He is not only transcendent over space but also over time. In other words, God is not confined to space nor limited by time. He is in the past, the present, and the future. He is in the past with the Israelites fleeing Egypt, present with us in our struggles, and in the future with us in glory as we worship him forever.

How We Got Here

Perhaps you're wondering, "Why are we getting a deep theological lesson on who God is?" It's a valid question, but allow me to give a valid answer. Before we can truly trust God in prayer—and before we can respond with patience—we must truly know God as he revealed himself in the Bible. Those were just three of his attributes!

Believer, I don't want you—or any of us—to simply know *about* God. I want us to *know* God. Knowing about God like you know the stats of your favorite athlete or how many Oscars your favorite actor has won will do you no good in the end. We must know God like we know our spouse or a beloved family member. We must know with affection—and we can't know with affection until we study him!

Trust God's Omnipotence

We may never actively think this, but how many times have we wrongfully thought there was a power struggle in Heaven? I'm sure we've all seen those silly memes on social media where Jesus and Satan are arm wrestling. That is simply unbiblical. There is no power struggle. God has Satan on a leash. So we must pray with that in mind. We're not praying to a God who doesn't obtain all control or is fighting off an equal match. We're praying to *the* God that uses his enemies as his footstool (Psalm 110:1). We're praying to *the* God that does whatever he pleases (Psalm 115:3). Our God is in control; our God is *the* sovereign one. Let that truth develop our patience.

Think of a time you prayed—however many times—for something to happen yet it didn't come to fruition. Perhaps it was a loved one fighting cancer; maybe it was for a big promotion that would allow you to provide more for your family. Or maybe it was as simple as praying a road trip to go smoothly. But then your prayer went unanswered. Your loved one succumbed to cancer; you didn't get the promotion; you got a flat tire halfway through the road trip and didn't have a spare. Had God lost control? Had Satan or one of his minions won the arm wrestling match? As the Apostle Paul likes to say, "By no means!"

The reason our prayers go unanswered is not because God ceased being all-powerful but because that's simply not the plan God had for us at that specific moment. He wants us to exercise patience. Sometimes it means we have to endure intense grief; oftentimes it's dealing with the major inconveniences of life. Either way, God is still with us and in control of our lives. And that's a good thing. Our lives would be in shambles if we were in control. We'd mess everything up (more than we already do). Thank God for the sovereignty of God.

Trust His Omniscience

Humans cannot see into the future, nor do we possess all knowledge—not even close. Billions of things occur in this universe that we don't know about—yet. Science may progress but it changes all the time. Humans will learn new extraordinary things only to get hung up on the next hindrance. We just don't know everything. And that's a great thing.

We must pray in light of God's omniscience. We can be so arrogant at times when we become frustrated with how a situation has played out. We think we were right. Even though we don't possess all knowledge, we were still pretty sure everything was falling into place. Though we prayed for something to happen, we didn't really need God's help. It would just happen.

And then it doesn't happen. And then we become agitated because, from our perspective, things aligned perfectly. When I first began dating my wife back in 2012, I told her my plan was to get married at 25, have our first child at 27 and our second at 29. Seemed like a great plan. Would you like to know what really happened? We got married at 22, first child at 24 and second at 26. I had everything planned—but God was way ahead of me.

The biblical response to this shouldn't be frustration or annoyance. May we never be frustrated or annoyed with our Creator. We must remember a vital, yet humbling truth: God is infinite; we are finite. He is the Creator; we are the creation. He possesses all knowledge; we know just a little bit (and even the little we know comes directly from him). The reality of God's omniscience should humble our hearts in prayer.

The next time God doesn't answer your prayer how you want, remember this comforting truth: God knows all things so you don't have to—so trust he's infinitely smarter than you. Have confidence that he has everything figured out. Believe he has a plan specifically *for you*.

Trust His Omnipresence

Humankind has attempted time travel many times. We see it in the movies and are enamored by it. It truly is fascinating. But there's just one problem: it's impossible. We can ponder the past and dream of the future, but can never go there. We live in the present—and only the present.

Praise be to God, he is not like us. God is "other" than us—completely holy. We must pray with God's omnipresence pervading our minds. There are countless times we've prayed for something only to see it's not what God wanted for us. In those moments we must remember he's already there. He is already where he will have us—and what he gives is always good. We don't need to be upset over unanswered prayer when we meditate on God's omnipresence, for it is then we know God not only knows the future, but he is already there—planning everything.

Trust Who God Is

At the most fundamental level, trusting God when our prayers go unanswered comes down to who we believe God is. If we believe he is who he says he is, then despair, frustration, or anger should never be a response to unanswered prayer. The only response should be trust and patience.

But we are planners—at least some are. We like to plan ahead and think of every possible outcome. It's easy to get wrapped up in every detail and have everything planned. James had something to say about our plans.

> Come now, you who say, 'Today or tomorrow we will go into such and such a town and spend a year there and trade and make a profit'— yet you do not know what tomorrow will bring. What is your life? For you are a mist that appears for a little time and then vanishes. Instead you ought to say, 'If the Lord wills, we will live and do this or that.' As it is, you boast in your arrogance. All such boasting is evil. So whoever knows the right thing to do and fails to do it, for him it is sin (James 4:13-17).

Is James condemning all planning? Is he telling us we should not plan for tomorrow or prepare for a family vacation? No, of course not. He is condemning the type of planning that leaves God out of the equation. It's a sinful, arrogant planning. A planning that forgets, neglects, or flat out ignores that we "are a mist that appears for a little time and then vanishes." It forgets that we do not know what tomorrow will bring. We may have a good idea of what tomorrow will be, but we can never know for certain. This is why we must trust God's plan and time.

Our first little girl, Jovi Grace, was born June 13, 2019—a complete month before her due date. That morning was just like any other. I woke up at 5:30 a.m., went into the living room to sip coffee and read Scripture. Next thing I know, at 6 a.m., my wife is calling my name. I walk into our room to her saying her water just broke.

A mere six hours later our daughter was born. Needless to say, I didn't expect that to happen. We were expecting a regular day since she was only 35 weeks and five days along, but God had other plans.

We can plan, but God sets them in stone.

We must remember that, "Many are the plans in the mind of a man, but it is the purpose of the Lord that will stand" (Proverbs 19:21). We can make plans all day long, but in the end, God's purpose will stand. The Roman guards would kill Jesus, but God's purpose of saving his people would stand. Joseph's brothers sold him into slavery, but God's plan for Joseph would stand.

Pray in Light of This

The Lord is good. He is good when he answers prayer and when he doesn't. For the times he doesn't, let us repent if our first inclination is to throw our hands up in frustration. Let us repent if it's easier to be mad at God than to trust him when our prayers aren't answered. What we believe about God determines how we respond when our prayers aren't answered how we'd like them to be.

Do we believe God is in control of our lives? If so, we must trust him when he doesn't give us what we want. We must trust him even when it doesn't make sense. Our trust in God should not be based on a particular situation but on who he is as God; which means whether he answers our prayers or not, we should trust him regardless because we know, according to the Bible, he withholds nothing good from us and will never forsake us.

There have been and will be many more times in your life that things don't make sense. Your prayer for a smooth road trip goes unanswered and now you are dealing with a flat tire on the interstate where things get dangerous. No matter how pointless it may feel, it never is. When our sinful hearts pull us to bitterness, let us yield to the Holy Spirit who calls us to thankfulness.

Let's leave the planning and timing in God's hand and just enjoy the ride in his arms.

Prayer of Reflection

Father, I struggle mightily with impatience. I get impatient with my spouse, my children, my job, and myself. I live a life of impatience. And yet, you call me to be patient. I know that, according to your Word, one of the sure signs I am trusting you is if I am waiting on you to work with patience. When I don't, it reveals I don't trust you to be God. Please help me. In Jesus's name, amen.

10

Lord, Sanctify Me

The Prayer God Always Answers

IF WORDS COULD truly melt your heart, it would be these from my daughter one day lying in bed. "Daddy," she said, "want to hold my hand?"

One of the great joys of my life is being a father. From playing on the swing to pushing them around in a wagon, being their dad brings me incredible happiness. Outside of my salvation and my wife, those two little girls are the best things that have ever happened to me.

And with two little girls—a three-year-old and a one-year-old—comes early mornings. One of those early mornings, however, came with an extra dose of God's grace in the form of a request. I get up at 5:30 a.m. every weekday. Then, I wake my wife up at 6 a.m. Most days, our oldest is awake by 6:30 a.m. but on one cold morning, she decided to bless us with her presence at 5:45 a.m.

It starts with a cry. "Mama! Mama! Mama!" she says until my wife opens her door. With eyes wide open, my daughter comes into our room and gets in our bed. When this happens, we let her watch early-morning TV. That morning, it happened to be *Monsters, Inc*. And here is the best part. As we both lie there in bed, habitually telling Jovi to lower her voice, I look over to see her hand stretched out and she said: "Daddy, will you hold my hand?"

"Yes, of course," I replied, with butterflies floating around in my stomach. How could I say no to that? Indeed, I cannot—I will not—say no to that. It doesn't matter if we're walking across the street, lying down in bed, or in a movie theater. If either of my children ask me to hold their hand, the answer will always be a heartfelt, "Yes!" They need not wonder what their daddy will say to that. No second-guessing, no reluctance, no worry. They will have the utmost confidence that I will always agree to hold their hands when they ask. Always.

The Prayer He Always Answers

Throughout this book we have talked about how God says no to us. Even more, we've gone over how to respond when he does say no. Whether it's with repentance, patience, trust, contentment, and the like, we know that our response to unanswered prayer reveals a lot about what we believe about God. And yet, we must talk about the opposite end of the spectrum.

God does say yes to us. In fact, there are several prayers that God will always—without reservation—say yes to. Just like I will always say yes to my daughter's request to hold hands, there are many prayer requests God will always answer in the affirmative. Though there are several requests God will answer time and time again, I want to focus on one: praying for our sanctification. Before we focus on our plea to be sanctified, let's turn our attention to the doctrine itself.

Sanctification: A Primer

The theological term is *sanctification*. In its simplest definition, sanctification refers to the process of becoming more and more like Jesus everyday.

Sinclair Ferguson, a teaching fellow at Ligonier Ministries and Chancellor's Professor of Systematic Theology at Reformed Theological Seminary, puts a beautiful spin on sanctification by saying:

> This is what 'sanctification' means: God has put his 'reserved' sign on something—temple vessels for example—or on someone who thereby becomes a 'saint', a person reserved for the Lord. He marks us out for his personal possession and use. We belong to him—and to nobody else, not even to ourselves. We come devoted to God.[39]

Sanctification, at its foundation, is the process by which Christians—those who've been bought by the precious blood of Jesus Christ—become more and more "devoted to God," as Ferguson writes. Sanctification is progressive, not instantaneous. "Sanctification," Dane Ortlund writes, "is lifelong, gradual growth in grace."[40] There are two key words here that are significant—*lifelong* and *gradual*.

Becoming more like Jesus does not happen overnight, though I am sure we all wish it did. I am not where I thought I would be as a Christian today. When God saved me years ago, I intended to be more holy, more Christlike, more godly than I am now. But I'm not. Not by a long shot.

---

[39] Sinclair Ferguson, *Devoted to God: Blueprints for Sanctification* (Edinburgh: Banner of Truth, 2016), 11.
[40] Dane Ortlund, *Deeper: Real Change for Real Sinners* (Wheaton: Crossway, 2021), 85.

Sometimes I get too angry; other times I'm a little too impatient. On many occasions my sarcasm comes too natural and my cynicism springs forth too often. I don't love my wife as I should and my love for the Lord wanes far too easily. In short, I'm less godly than I planned to be now.

Wherever you are in your walk with Jesus—whether it's been a month, a couple years, or decades—I imagine you feel the same way. We all do. We all get discouraged with our progress. We all are prone to frustration, realizing we are not as godly as we should be. But sanctification, like the growing of trees and plants—as theologian John Owen puts it—takes time. It's slow, boring, and not easily seen.

If you watch grass grow you won't see progress. After awhile, you'll become impatient and annoyed that the grass seems to remain the same length. But if you mow your lawn and check it after a week, you'll notice it's grown so much where you need to mow again.

So it is with the Christian life. So it is with grace in sanctification. If you are experiencing minuscule growth in your walk with Christ, don't become discouraged, frustrated, or annoyed. There is certainly value in some discouragement simply because you shouldn't be complacent. However, don't despair. God is still molding you, still shaping you, still forming you into the image of Christ.

He is going to sanctify us until the day we die, because until we pass away, our flesh will need to be shed. We must be patient, we must be steadfast, and we must be focused.

If I look back to a year ago, I don't see much change, and it can be discouraging. If I, however, look back to who I was before getting saved, there's a world of difference. And it's all by the grace of God.

If You Ask, He Will Answer.

There will never be a moment in our lives when God says no to us praying to be made more like his Son. That's part of why we're still on this side of heaven. God could've plucked us all up and we could be in glory now. But that's not what God planned. He ordained for us to be used by him—and what a privilege that is!

Further, we must not be afraid to pray that prayer. We all want God to make us more like Jesus but much of sanctification comes to us through the avenue of suffering. Much of sanctification may happen via our response to unanswered prayer. At the end of the day, we must not despise our suffering or unanswered prayer, for it makes us more like Jesus. We are made more like Jesus through our pruning. This is the end goal: to be like Christ (Romans 8:29). Everything that happens to us in this life is used by God to mold us more into the image of his Son. Our suffering is the road to our glorification one day. Remember the example of Jesus in Philippians 2, the great chapter on his humility. Jesus "humbled himself by becoming obedient to the point of death, even death on a cross" (Philippians 2:8).

Jesus experienced the ultimate suffering through his life and death on the cross.

> Therefore, God has highly exalted him and bestowed on him the name that is above every name, so that at the name of Jesus every knee should bow, in heaven and on earth and under earth, and every tongue confess that Jesus Christ is Lord, to the glory of God the Father (vv. 9–11).

Jesus's suffering on earth is the very path that led to his exaltation in heaven.

In the same vein, our suffering will, one day sooner than we realize, lead to our glorification, our exaltation, our glorious "inheritance that is imperishable, undefiled, and unfading, kept in heaven for [us]" (1 Peter 1:4). Therefore, Christian, keep your eyes fixated on the glories of heaven. Heavenly glory won't take the pain of suffering away, but it will make it worth it. It will be worth it because God will sanctify you in the process.

Prayer of Reflection

Lord, I know the path to being more sanctified often comes through the valleys of unanswered prayer. That is what it's all about—becoming more like your Son. I know that if I ask you to make me more like Jesus, you will. Help me remember that means you might use unanswered prayer as a means by which you mold me more into his likeness. In Jesus's name, amen.

Conclusion
Our Good, His Glory

THE WHOLE MESSAGE of this book is centered on our response to unanswered prayer. God tells us no often, and we are responsible for responding in a godly manner.

Ultimately, God tells us no for two reasons: our good and his glory.

Our Good

We think we know what's best for us. We look out for our own good and, most of the time, we're pretty sure of what that looks like. When life is a breeze, when the bills are paid, when our health is great—that's our "good." In our mind, that's what is best for us. But that's not always God's "good" for us. And if we are honest, we know that too.

As Christians, we can rest assured that God is for our good (Romans 8:28). That "good" doesn't translate into a carefree life. It's not as simple as the popular phrase, "Live,

Laugh, Love." Many things that are for our good won't necessarily *feel* good. God doesn't call us to live lives that feel good. He's called us to live lives that are worthy of the gospel—and that will involve pain.

When my wife and I experienced our own pain of unanswered prayer in the introduction, life was incredibly difficult. We had never gone through something of that magnitude. My wife had been in a near-fatal wreck in high school, and I bumped my head once that caused a large bump on my forehead, which turned me into a unicorn for a month, but nothing more significant than that. When I was told the news of the blighted ovum, my brain assented but still didn't register for days. As my wife sobbed for days, of course I comforted her, but I didn't cry—and I can sometimes be an emotional person. The tears weren't there. I was incredibly sad, but it was as if I was numb to the news. And though I knew God was good, that still didn't mean I couldn't cry. But I didn't. Not until it finally happened.

I tell you this story, friend, to tell you of God's goodness to us in the midst of it. It was a deeply painful trial, but wasn't without God's sanctifying grace in our lives. God worked through and in us while we grieved, wept, and stood puzzled. Our "good" involved working through this suffering, this trial, this heartache. Though painful it was, the pain doesn't compare to the deep and abiding joy and triumph of knowing we are in Christ and our Heavenly Father is working to make us more like his Son.

I imagine you're going through some type of trial right now. And in that trial you've prayed continually, but to no avail. God keeps telling you no. And you're becoming frustrated, disheartened, and afraid. Why isn't God answering your prayers for deliverance, for relief, for success? Ultimately—and thankfully—we don't need to know why. That's why it's important to focus on our response. But what we do know, as a fact, is that he is for our good and his glory. So don't become disheartened. God is for you. Though your trial is fierce and your pain is great, God is working and he is for you. That's all that matters.

His Glory

God's glory matters above all else. That's the end game of the Christian life. We want to be successful—to God's glory. We want to eat and drink—to God's glory. We want to do all things, as Paul says—to God's glory. The desire to see God glorified should overpower our insecurities, fears, and frustrations related to unanswered prayer. God caring about his glory most of all is the best news in the world. His glory is beautiful, transcendent, and better than life.

Christian, God is for you and his glory. If you habitually remind yourself of that—even in the darkest of days—unanswered prayer won't be so painful because you know, no matter what the outcome, that God has you in his arms and you are secure in him.

Rest easy.

Acknowledgments

THIS BOOK wouldn't have been written without the loving, caring sacrifice of my wife, Shale. She puts up with a lot!

I'd also like to thank Alex Duke, who made sure I didn't sound like a dufus and to John Manning who did a fantastic job (as always) on the cover and interior of the book.

And to my elders at Sovereign Grace Bible Church: thank you for your leadership and insights that went into this book. Above all, I'm thankful to God for his immeasurable grace in giving me the ability to write this work.

Bibliography

D. Martyn Lloyd-Jones, *Studies in the Sermon on the Mount* (Grand Rapids: Eerdmans, 1960), vol. 1, 38.

Dane Ortlund, *Deeper: Real Change for Real Sinners* (Wheaton: Crossway, 2021), 85.

Dean Inserra, *Getting Over Yourself: Trading Believe-In-Yourself Religion for Christ-Centered Christianity* (Chicago: Moody Publishers, 2021) 84.

Desiring God, "Piper: 'God is always doing 10,000 things in your life, and you may be aware of 3 of them.'" *Twitter.* November 8, 2012. https://twitter.com/desiringgod/status/266584993881550849

Don Currin. (2021, December 6). *Contentment is an embracing of the sovereignty of God; working all things after the counsel of his will and not ours.* [Status update]. Facebook. https://www.facebook.com/profile.php?id=100007533195852

Donald S. Whitney, *Spiritual Disciplines for the Christian Life* (Colorado Springs: NavPress, 2014), 25.

Garrett Kell, "When God Says No to Your Earnest Prayers."

The Gospel Coalition, September 24, 2020. https://www.thegospelcoalition.org/article/god-says-no-earnest-prayers/.

J.I. Packer, *Knowing God* 20th Anniversary edition (Downers Grove: IVP Books, 193), 97.

J.I. Packer, *Knowing God* 20th Anniversary Edition (Downers Grove: IVP Books, 1993), 206-207.

Jared C. Wilson, *Supernatural Power for Everyday People: Experiencing God's Extraordinary Spirit in Ordinary Life* (Nashville: Thomas Nelson, 2018), 66.

John Macarthur and Richard Mayhue ed., *Biblical Doctrine: A Systematic Summary of Bible Truth* (Wheaton: Crossway, 2017), 513.

John Piper, *Desiring God: Meditations of a Christian Hedonist* (Colorado Springs: Multnomah, 1983), 32.

Kevin Halloran, *When Prayer is a Struggle: A Practical Guide for Overcoming Obstacles in Prayer* (Phillipsburg: P&R Publishing Company, 2021), 74.

R.C. Sproul, *Chosen by God: Knowing God's Perfect Plan of His Glory and His Children* (Carol Stream: Tyndale House Publishers, 1986) 16.

RC Sproul, *The Invisible Hand: Do All Things Really Work for Good?* (Phillisburg: P&R Publishing, 1996), 10.

R.C. Sproul. "Perfectly Human." TableTalk Magazine, December 2015.

RC Sproul, *Truths We Confess: A Systematic Exposition of the Westerminster Confession of Father* (Sanford: Reformation Trust, 2019). 283.

RC Sproul, https://www.ligonier.org/learn/devotionals/asking-seeking-knocking

Sinclair Ferguson, *Devoted to God: Blueprints for Sanctification* (Edinburgh: Banner of Truth, 2016), 11.

Timothy Keller, *Prayer: Experiencing Awe and Intimacy with God* (New York: Penguin Books, 2014), 45.

Timothy Keller, *Prayer: Experiencing Awe and Intimacy with God* (New York: Penguin Books, 2014), 226.

Timothy Keller, *Prayer: Experiencing Awe and Intimacy with God* (New York: Penguin Books, 2014), 237.

Thomas Watson, *The Doctrine of Repentance* 7th Edition *(Edinburgh: Banner of Truth, 2016), 13.*

More from Blake Long

Available on Amazon

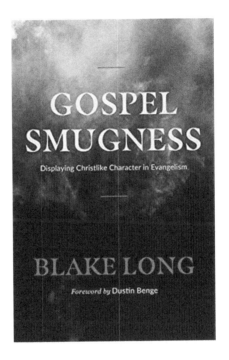

My blog, Theology & Life, exists to help everyday Christians not only understand theological concepts but how they impact our daily lives.

Go to theology-and-life.com to read!

Made in the USA
Columbia, SC
22 April 2023